THE HOUSE ON DOGBONE ST.

THE STORY OF A RESILIENT WOMAN WHO OVERCOMES LIMITATIONS, BREAKS GENERATIONAL ABUSES AND ULTIMATELY TRIUMPHS

JULIA DUTHIE

CONTENTS

For Dilys

FOREWORD

Endurance is a gift not afforded to most, but, to Author Julia Duthie, it seems to have been given in abundance. I say this because of the content of this magnificent memoir, a truthful rendition in all its haphazardness, which has fueled her existence from childhood to the current day. Although the House on Dogbone St. describes the life of Julia, I can bet that there are aspects of the book we could all relate to. Whether we personally experienced the unfavourable cards that life sometimes dealt, or not, this story will pull at the heartstrings of those who also witnessed these occurrences with others that crossed their paths. A life teacher, hope keeper, and adversity cheater are what Julia Duthie is, in all its abundance. Overall, her story is a reflection of a life that has moulded her into the woman she is today. It is, therefore, a must-read, as even through the most treacherous of times, she has proven that circumstances do not have to end with unfavourable results.

ROLLING STONES

We moved six times by the time I was seven years old. Although this is not the most interesting part of my early life, it is a fact I like to mention, as it implies a life on the run. Given the frequency and regularity of packing up and moving on, I guess to a degree, we were always running. Dad often said that mum made trouble and we had to leave, which I always found incongruent to the scant memories I have of her. She didn't seem to do much of anything other than cry, which she did a lot. It wasn't even that we moved very far each time, so I'm not sure what good packing up and leaving so frequently did. I mean, it can't have been possible to wipe the slate completely clean each time, could it? Moving house annually had some benefits though, as it created the perfect timeline for my memories. With each new house, I can pinpoint the exact year, like a mental Rolodex of every early childhood experience. At five years old? Oh yes, that was in so and so house and I was attending so and so school, etc. It was a very helpful check and balance as memories can sometimes play tricks.

It all began within a small semi-detached starter home in a tiny cul-de-sac. Nestled shyly behind a petrol station, you would have to know it was there, as I almost missed it myself when as an adult, I went to see where my family's story began. The town of my birth is of no particular note. It defines itself as a commuter town in that it has a mainline station to Waterloo, is positioned conveniently between the South East's main arterial motorways and you can access both Heathrow and Gatwick within half an hour. You could say that it's a great place to get away from, but for me, it has been my home for over 50 years. I know almost every inch of it, such that, should I ever need to become a cabbie, I could pass "the knowledge" test in no time. Apart from its transport links, it also has other charms. A beautiful park, theatre, cinema complex, shopping centre and various High St. branded shops and eateries are amongst them. It is typical of any suburban town in leafy Surrey, and to all outward appearances, my early life within it would have seemed middle-class and affluent. It has recently enjoyed (or perhaps endured) a makeover, and can now be seen far and wide as 30-story apartment buildings rise like glass and concrete overlords, not dissimilar to HG Wells War of the Worlds' aliens that stand proudly as statues in homage to the town's links to his great literary works.

I was, even by 1970's standards, a small baby. I weighed a tiny 6 pounds and according to my dad, my mum, who had previously given birth to an 11-pounder, just kept pushing, even though I was out. More significant than my stealthy entry into this world was that once she had realised her mistake (and I use this word deliberately), she asked for me to be taken away as I was so small that she refused to hold me "in case I would break". This was the story that dad told me when I was a child, and I would giggle at the thought of my mum huffing and puffing away with everyone wondering what on earth for. However, as I grew older the story got darker. "From the moment of your first breath, your mother never held you, fed you, changed you or looked at you with anything other than blank indifference," he said. Looking back, I think he was trying to tell me how well he'd done raising us on his own, and yes, those early years must have been hard on him as was the enormity of me learning at that moment that my mother had rejected me at birth. I was the third in line, following behind my elder brothers aged three and six, with my younger sister arriving just 16 months after me. Having had perfect three-year gaps between my elder siblings and I, dad joked that my younger sister "slipped out", which I suppose had the double meaning of being an "accident". To me, it implied that if mum was indifferent to me, then by the time my younger sister arrived, she must have practically gone unnoticed.

With his "brood" intact, it was off to the next house. Here, we lived next to Maggie. Dad had many sayings over the years, "what's the fuss?" when I hurt myself, "no money" which he said if I wanted him to buy me something, but his most used phrase was, "ask Maggie" when I'd ask him a question he didn't want to answer or was too busy. Maggie lived next door and dad said she was very fond of my mum. Given that I'd heard so many good things about her over the years, and the fact that she was someone who actually knew my mum, when I was old enough to contact her myself, I did indeed "Ask Maggie". I wanted to know what it was like for mum back then. What was it like for me? I was hoping she would reassure me that things weren't as bad, that somehow my imaginings built around the stories I'd heard had been exaggerated over time, but sadly, over a very long and emotional afternoon, she confirmed that if anything, the stories had been played down. We talked a lot about my mum's condition and how worried she was about her. It was obvious to everyone that my mum was clinically depressed, in fact, Maggie thought I had depression too, as I didn't chatter like most toddlers, but instead, sat staring in my high-chair, silent and disengaged. She would do what she could, letting herself into our house and tending to our needs, with mum oblivious to our cries and to Maggie's presence. She found my mother's disengagement very distressing and would do what she could to encourage a bond, but it was hopeless. With dad at work each day, her biggest fear was that we would hurt ourselves. My younger sister and I were largely contained in either play pens, cots or highchairs, but my elder brothers were free to roam. Dad maintained that he was at work with the heavy implication that it was under mum's watch when his eldest son pulled a full saucepan of gravy onto himself, resulting in his skin melting like a meat mudslide from shoulder to waist. Maggie begged dad to take the child to the hospital for skin grafts, but he was not one for doctors, so my brother's skin stayed where it was, molten and pitted, forever a reminder of that awful event.

We left the watchful eye of Maggie after just over a year and moved across town. It was a lovely, quiet cul-de-sac. The road was flanked by a cow field, and I have very few but fond memories of it. Early in the spring, there was an enormous amount of rain that flooded the field. I have a clear memory of the cows' being replaced by a man in a canoe, passing down the end of my road. The house itself was small but very pretty, with white cladding and a curved lawn in the front. I have a picture of me sitting on my dad's lap, and there was a white conch-like shell just outside the front door which we still have to this day. I remember attending a nursery school nearby and have vague memories of warm milk in tiny little bottles with tin foil caps. It's a shame that kids these days won't know the pleasure of popping the top off and licking the cream on the underside. I recounted this memory to my kids when they were little, and they said, "we know all about that mum – Margaret Thatcher the milk snatcher". Funny how an entire political career can be summarised in the minds of children! We must have stayed a short while here as when we were a little older, my sister and I walked to a nursery at the local primary school each day via the alleyways. I think my mum was at home for some time during this period, but I only really remember my dad dropping us off at the gate. I think we walked back home, which sounds outrageous now, but it was the 1970s after all, so probably not that unusual.

Our primary school was a wonderful Victorian red-bricked affair. If I close my eyes, I can still literally recall almost every part of it. It had the typical main hall which held assemblies and sports, and the oblig-atory (still used in schools today), climbing frames that were wheeled into place and then clamped into hidden hooks on the floor. I always found this to be mesmerising. It was like watching robot arms glide across the floor and 'dock', much like a space probe returning from its mission. There was the imposing 'horse' which was made up of four layers with a leather top, and it looked massive whichever height they set it to. There was also the ever-present smell of scented sawdust held in a red bucket, in case nerves, tummy bugs or aversion to school dinners required it to be duly sprinkled. There was a large playground to the front, which had a concrete structure in the shape of a cat's head. You could run up on it and sit astride it or hide underneath, with running up the side being the hardest challenge. Those who made it to the tip of the ears were rewarded with a higher status amongst the mere mortals who could only imagine such heady heights. There were metal bars for the girls to spin around on, plus best of all, there was a shelter filled with rubber car tyres. Although the tyres were essentially just rolled around the playground, it was endless fun. It's hard to imagine in this 'Health and Safety' era, any of these items being sanctioned today. It was literally 'concrete meets steel' everywhere, but I loved it. The rear of the school had even more metal climbing apparatus with extra concrete to cushion your falls. There was also a large, grassed area where we would make daisy chains in the summer, and those that could (not me), would cart-wheel from one end to the next. I was particularly interested in the art room which was in a wooden building. The smell of wet acrylic and clay was deli-cious, and if I even catch a whiff of these things today, I am instantly transported back to my days at school.

Memories are very clear from this time which some may find remarkable, but I recall many 'major' events at this school - major that is, to a little girl. My most profound memory is being acutely aware that I couldn't manage gymnastics. I tried and tried but couldn't even accomplish a forward roll. Little girls around me were doing 'crabs', cartwheels and handstands, and I couldn't even tuck my chin under and roll. This did, however, present my very first opportunity to join the boys' foot-ball classes. There was just one small problem, I had no football boots! I'm not sure where they came from, maybe lost property, but I proudly joined the squad with a pair of red trainers. Out of school memories are also vivid. There was one occasion when there was a horrendous storm with vertical rain and ear-splitting thunder. Walking home meant leaving the school gates, taking a right down a main road, past the first and second set of shops and then all the way to our home. It's not an insignificant distance when you're a little girl. We were absolutely drenched and hoarse from screaming. And having banged furiously at the front door, we were very relieved to find Carole or "Arole" as our home help was known, standing there to greet us. I can't remember how many days she was with us, or even how she came to be with us. I'm not sure if Home Helps even exist anymore, but I'm assuming we needed one, even though mum was home, so there she was. Carole was wonderful! She scooped us up and towelled us down as we were drenched with rain water. We also made hats together, and I can remember making a fez. It's funny what one can remember from early childhood days.

On our way to nursery, there was a lady we would see who had a Chow. I thought this was perhaps the most beautiful dog I'd ever seen. It was like a bear with a lion's mane and a huge black nose. I've since found out that they are quite aggressive dogs, which seems a bit of a wicked trick of nature given that it also looks so primped and coiffed. Perhaps, that's why it was so cross? Anyway, this dog was owned by a lady who looked like Mrs. Bucket (pronounced 'bouquet' just in case you haven't seen 'Keeping Up Appearances'). She wore a silk scarf over her enormous 'do' and was ever so posh. She epitomised the theory that owners looked like their dogs. Come to think of it, she wasn't terribly friendly either. There are smells that take me back to this house. They ought to be of baked cakes, fresh, out-of-the-oven bread, or perhaps bacon, but the first smell that takes me back in an instant is that of rotting flesh. I didn't know what it was the first time I smelt it. In fact, it's a smell that is almost lost to me now. I'm talking about the humble hedgehog, or more precisely the humble dead hedgehog. It troubles me that kids today, (a) probably won't see a live one and (b) won't have the wonder of poking a dead one. Riddled with fleas and almost 'alive' with maggots, this was fascinating.

It was at this school and at the tender age of four that I made my first friend. Sitting cross-legged on the floor of the classroom, I suddenly felt a flood of warmth. My soon-to-be bestie had wet her knickers. She was either terrified of asking to go to the loo or had not quite mastered the timing. Whatever the reason for her mishap, it allowed a moment of bonding between us, and we became friends. I met her mum shortly after having been invited to my very first play date. I was to have tea at their home, a house I walked by every day on my way to school, which I must admit was very grand. It was a double-fronted large Victorian house, set back from the road with a sweeping front driveway which housed a red Citroen and a white Jaguar with room for at least six more cars. The large oak door led into a traditional black and white tiled entrance which framed a grand Victorian staircase to the first floor. To the back of the house was a conservatory. This might be a run-of-the-mill add-on today, but in 1974 it was very progressive. Just off the conservatory was the 'white room'. Everything in it was white. There was a leather suite, white carpet and a beautiful piano. It was also out of bounds to kids as was the 'black room'. This was literally the negative of the white room with a black sofa and carpet and the largest hi-fi system I had ever seen. It's only now that I look back in awe at this house, as at the age of four, these material things were lost on me. I did, however, adore my bestie's mum, and so began a life-long maternal friendship. She was, and still is, a remarkable woman, a trained chartered accountant, businessperson, magazine editor, shop owner, homemaker, mother and now CEO of a large housing development company. She is probably the only person, other than my immediate family, to remain constant to this day. I say this because she has come to my aid on many occasions over the years.

Life on this road was brief, and in the main, quite uneventful. However, after just one year, it was time to move on again, to a non- descript terraced house closer to dad's work at the local Borough Council and almost in the heart of the town centre. It may have been a stone's throw from his work, but it was some distance to school. The walk to our primary school was probably one and a half miles or more. It was a nice walk though, which took us through the park. The summer months were wonderful, the winter less so. I remember walking with my brothers to school and I was so cold when I got there that the Headteacher invited me into her office to warm up, and while my toes regained feeling, she poured me a cup of tea to defrost the rest of my body. I wonder if these little acts of kindness happen in primary schools today. I hope that in today's hectic and 'hands-off' times, head teachers take the time to notice the need for extra attention with certain pupils. I remember feeling terribly special when I received this act of kindness.

Other memories from this time was the proximity to Mackenzie's field which was our main playground. My eldest brother had lots of friends, one of which was the captain of the revered Mackenzie''s field football team. I tagged along quite a bit to see if I could get involved with their games which wasn't ideal for them, given that, I was five and they were eleven, but nonetheless, I was included in some things. I was particularly proud to be asked to help paint an abandoned greenhouse set in overgrown bushes in the field. I was so keen to make a good impression on the older boys that I painted the up-and-down strokes so carefully, my arms nearly fell off with the effort. Given this demonstration of my usefulness, I was asked to perform another task for my now new 'master's'. One such assignment was to take a dustbin bag full of conkers home. No problem, I thought, I just need to carefully drag the bag home down the street, until...I realised that the bag felt kind of light?" The horror of discovering that a complete bag of scrumped conkers that had taken a whole afternoon to collect were now dashed in a crazed zigzag, left me stricken. Suffice to say, my membership to the big kid's club was terminated without notice.

In 1976, we moved again, this time across town to be closer to my grandparents. The new area we moved to was then and still is predominantly Muslim. I was very much amongst the minority in my new school, but at just six years of age, you don't notice such things. I just had a lot of friends with unfamiliar names. We lived in a much larger house than we had before. Our new home was one of those Victorian semis with original features. It had a front room, dining room, kitchen (with breakfast bar and larder), three bedrooms, a bathroom, and a study. It was very sizeable by our previous standards. It was also just a five minute walk to school and to my grandparent's house. They lived just up the road in an unremarkable one-bedroom flat which must have been quite an adjustment from their earlier lives in India. I still drive past it from time to time and can't believe they lived there, as it's so tiny. I can picture every inch of it from the front room to their 'burgundy' bedroom (there must have been a cheap deal on burgundy paint as they even painted the ceilings with it). They had a small corridor with a grandfather clock, a stuffed yellow canary in a blue box and a small stone bulldog that acted as a doorstop. Their kitchen had a yellow table with two matching chairs, and the back door went straight out to a little garden. The house had a peculiar smell that only old peoples' homes seem to have; a combination of dust and Steradent. I would track back behind the row of houses that separated us, go to the back door and let myself in. Grandad was always pleased to see me, granny less so. By the age of six, you are much more aware of the world around you. I think this may be why memories are much stronger around this age. On the one hand, I had wonderful memories of friends who I met through school and who came to my sixth birthday party in June of 1976. This was the famous year of drought, and I clearly remember peeling the skin off my shoulders, which I found fascinating, collecting water from a standpipe in the street and pouring saucepans of water into the cistern of the toilet to make it flush. I also remember the day I got shot in the stomach with my neighbour's air rifle. There was an audible 'crack' accompanying an invisible hand punching me in the gut, followed by a tiny pellet-sized black bruise appearing on my tanned little tummy. My dad was furious and went straight next door to talk to the family. They were Italian and mostly kept to themselves. The 'gunman' was one of the sons who I really liked, and I felt sorry for him as my dad "gave him what for!" This may conjure up images of a big burly man going next door to protect his young, but dad was a very slight man, not prone to any machismo behaviour, so I suppose this would have been very unusual. I think after everything, everyone was just happy that nothing worse than a tiny bruise on my belly had occurred. I, on the other hand, was rather proud to have survived being shot!

I have memories I'm ashamed of, such as the day I scooped out all my dad's tropical fish onto the carpet. To this day, I'm not sure why I did that. Perhaps it was just to get attention or maybe I thought they were getting too much of the attention I was looking for and was jealous. It could even be that I was just curious to see what would happen. The more likely reason could have been that I was just bored. I used to walk home from school all alone at 3.00 pm and let myself into the house. Given that dad wouldn't be home until around 6.00 pm, and mum was mostly in the hospital, this made for quite a lot of time to kill (quite literally!) Whatever the motive, this was not my best moment, and I do feel bad for the carnage I caused. There also the day my eldest brother and I burnt down the shed with a fire constructed from a Bonio dog biscuit box. It wasn't intentional, of course, as we were hoping just to burn the box; however, the entire plastic corrugated shed melted before our eyes. With nothing to be done but marvel at the thick acrid smoke that snaked into the sky above, we found ourselves quite helpless and felt pretty guilty.

We may be coming across as rogues, but we were always polite and respectful to others even if not terribly so in our own home. We had a cream faux leather sofa for example. For a short while, it looked quite nice in that the material was wipe-clean, so the sofa could manage whatever detritus we could inflict on it. It wasn't terribly comfy though, especially if you had little legs that couldn't secure themselves on the floor to prevent you from slipping off. I don't think we can blame its demise on our bare feet, but the repeated stabbing of forks into the upholstery, that at first caused discrete little holes, ultimately mashing it to shreds. I wish it stopped there, but I also remember cutting off one side of the table legs on our solid oak coffee table to make a slide. There were more serious misdemeanours too, including shutting the glass door on purpose as one of our friends ran through the hall-way. This ended in him crashing straight through it and being rushed to the hospital due to the invention of safety glass being some years off.

Although not a violent man, dad was exasperated by these antics, and typically, for the day, he had a measure of control over his four wild offspring by implementing capital punishment. This was mostly managed with a sharp stroke of the cane or slipper. Hard to imagine now, but this was the seventies and I'm not saying it wasn't deserved! Something less deserved was our being locked in our room overnight from 7:00 pm to 7:00 am, with wooden bars on our windows preventing any kind of escape. An old-fashioned commode served as our en-suite facility. Whether this was for our safety or his convenience is something I can only wonder about.

During our stay in this house was a time when the extent of my mum's illness first became clear to me. Whether it was because the incidents became more extreme, or that my six-year-old self was starting to piece things together, the memories from this time are strong. Although mum was home from time to time, there were long periods of her absence where she would go "for a rest". Other than that, I don't recall much else from her until the day the emergency services came. It had started as a normal day at primary school. We had gone on a field trip to the local park and collected leaves to put into our scrapbooks. I had walked home by myself, as usual, and as I turned left into our road, I saw fire engines, police cars and an ambulance. I ran the last few metres and rushed through the front door to find a huddle of adults around my mum in the front room. Thankfully, there was no fire, crime or accident to deal with. It turns out that mum was just lonely so she gave them a call. It was all very dramatic, and whether directly related to this incident or not, after nine short months, we were on the move once more.

April 15th, 1977, you might wonder how I know the moving date of our final resting place. Well, it was my two older brother's birthdays, and annoyingly to them, it fell on the same day. How they felt about spending their 10th and 13th birthdays, lugging wooden tea chests, is anyone's guess. At seven years old, I'm sure I was more focused on the prospect of making new friends in the street, navigating another new school and exploring our new home. House number 6 had three bedrooms. I say three, but really it was two and a half. Dad, of course, bagged the main bedroom and my two brothers naturally claimed the other, leaving my sister and I relegated to the box room. We didn't need much space as we brought very little with us, and given our previous experience, we probably thought we wouldn't be stopping long. Our bedroom was not actually a bedroom at all, but a storage room that was only wide enough to wedge two single beds together. It housed a broken oil heater in the corner that had a small shelf on which to place our worldly goods. There were no cupboards, drawers or carpet, and the whole left side was slick with black mould. Although there were no bars on the windows, this cold, damp, cramped space felt like a big climb-down.

Our road was a typical suburban cul de sac, and dad would have felt very proud to have afforded to move his family to such a pretty tree-lined street. Filled with 1930's-built bungalows, each with manicured front gardens, it was every inch a typical middle-class enclave. There were many young affluent families living there, and our home was placed directly in the middle of a stretch between two roundabouts which the kids affectionately referred to as the "Dogbone", given its resemblance to a Bonio dog biscuit. Our bungalow was set on a large plot, with over 100 ft of garden, housing a large well-kept lawn, rose bushes, a selection of tree cover and best of all, a coal bunker! Right at the back was an overgrown section that had the remnants of a compost heap and a large broken-down shed. The previous owners were elderly and had sold up to end their days in a retirement home. It had clearly been loved once, as the garden was full of life and was clean and welcoming, but it was evident that as their previous occupants had aged, so had the house. I'd like to imagine that it was quite pleased with its new young family and all the potential energy they might bring.

We settled in over the coming days and made friends with the kids on the road. In typical 70's style, we played out all day, and with the school just around the corner and having two playing fields, we had plenty of outdoor opportunities. Before long, we were fully installed, well not quite fully because mum didn't come with us this time.

ASK MAGGIE

Mum was now a full time patient in a mental institution. According to my dad, she checked herself into the hospital. I guess she may have contributed to this outcome and sectioned herself, but I'm not completely sure about this fact. If she hadn't done it herself, I'm pretty certain someone would have done it for her sooner or later. The hospital she was admitted to was a classic Victorian mental institution. I say it was because it is now a sprawling housing estate complete with a Buddhist temple and a Sainsbury's. Back then though, it was the sort of place that resembled the mental institution in 'One Flew Over the Cuckoo's Nest' which it could easily be based on. I visited it a few times and always found the nurses to be very nice. We would have rolls of ice cream wrapped in paper, which I've never had before, or since. We were always taken to the kitchens by the staff, probably to protect us from the sights, sounds and smells of the patients. I don't recall being particularly uncomfortable there. As kids do, you make the best of things, and the ice cream was a trump card in diversion.

I can't say I was upset by my mum being away because my world at seven years old was quite a simple one. I loved school! In fact, I never missed a single day of my Primary and Middle School education. I had wonderful friends there, and specifically, I was part of the 'J' club that was made up of Jackie, Jo and myself. We had badges and passwords and took our membership very seriously. I excelled at music and art and I loved all team sports, as I was particularly good at football rounders, netball and hockey. As there was no homework at this time, my home life didn't affect my studies. Although not a scholar, I held my own in all the academic classes and I loved my teachers. I have to admit that my art teacher was my favourite. She was big-busted, warm, and caring, and I loved everything about her which made what happened all the more mortifying.

It started as a normal art lesson, in that, I sat down on my tiny wooden chair and set to work on whatever crayon creation I would produce that day. All was well but soon turned to a catastrophe as my clean white page was soiled by a head lice that had fallen from my scalp. Most kids, I assume, would never know the incomparable feeling of having literally hundreds of the critters swarming around their hair, but when they are left to multiply unchecked, they literally run out of room and fall out. My teacher must have seen the offending louse and insisted, there and then, to give my hair a little brush through. I may have been slight, but I was also as tough as a lioness with a matted blonde mane to match, so when the hairbrush came close to revealing my embarrassing secret, I just instinctively slapped her in the face. I was braced for her wrath, but rather than being sent to the headteacher for the standard 1970's-style punishment, she apologised manically and guided me to the school nurse's office. I felt terrible about the whole incident but knew that if she'd gotten any closer, she would see that I was teeming with them.

If you have a lot of lice, they lose some of their repulsiveness that only familiarity can bring. My sister and I would while away the hours picking them out of each other's hair and putting them into a Tupperware container in front of us. Nowadays, you need to comb through the hair with a special nit comb only to find the occasional louse. When you have a lot and they're allowed to grow to their full, blood-bloated potential, you can feel them and pull them out. There is nothing more satisfying in fact, than getting a big one between your fingertips and rolling it until it's, or more accurately, your blood comes out with an audible "click".

Nit control was largely managed by the school nurse, but at home, we were left to do our own laundry. Keeping our clothes clean was undoubtedly a relative concept. I can't seem to get my teenage kids to put their dirty clothes in the laundry basket let alone wash, dry and iron them. Every Sunday night, I would do my best to make my battered uniform presentable with a combination of hand washing and spray starch, quite how I smelled to others I can only guess. There were some clues though. For instance, there was a family that lived directly opposite our house; made up of a mum, a dad and two boys. The mum was tall with dark hair and she was very striking. Although the eldest son was a couple of years older than me, the younger one was my age and we attended the same school. He wasn't the most dynamic of boys but he was kind and had lots of cool stuff. For example, he was one of the first kids to get a skateboard and a Raleigh Chopper Bike. His family also had a caravan called a Sprite, and quite unusual for the 1970's, a car - an orange/beige Triumph Toledo. I don't think his dad thought too much of the wayward family across the road, but he never said anything directly. It was more his look of disapproval that I recall.

His mum was a different story. She was always

happy to see me and there was one act of kindness that I will never forget. Parkas were all the rage around 1977, and I probably nagged my dad to get one for me. Mine was the classic blue with orange lining. It had a furry hood and a little strap on the top, to shorten or lengthen the hood depth as desired. They've probably been banned by the Health and Safety Executive now, as you literally had no peripheral vision at all, which was interesting when crossing roads. I loved this jacket, but after a few months of constant use, the orange lining had turned a mottled brown and was definitely none too fragrant. However, as if by magic, I came home with something looking and smelling brand new, so I deemed it miraculous. My friend's mum, with such deftness, had asked me for my coat as I went in, washed and dried it in time before I went home and never mentioned it again.

Shoes were another issue. I may have had a brand-new parka, but in the main, most of my limited wardrobe was previously owned by my older brother. Hand-me-down clothes were one thing, and second-hand shoes from your brother who is three years your senior are another. They were passed to me sometimes after they had started life with the brother before him, so, they were not only massive, but also quite battered. However, I managed to fit my tiny little toes into them with a bit of inventiveness. I worked out that if I put newspaper into the toe area, they would at least stay on. It seemed like a perfect solution, provided that I changed the paper often. There must have been some money for shoes though, as I can remember the one time that my dad bought me a pair of Gola black and gold trainers. Oh, my goodness, how beautiful they were! So beautiful, in fact, that I would put them back in the box every night and slide them under my bed. I was so excited about them that I would run to school just to prove to myself that they made me run faster and were therefore to be loved all the more. Gola shoes aside, my wardrobe was extremely limited. I had a pair of skin-tight jeans, a yellow roll-neck jumper and my parka. Everything was always dirty and always either too small or too large to which I earned the quite reasonable nickname of 'Scruffy Duffy'. Well, kids are wonderful that way.

There were other neighbours within our road who started to feature in my daily life. There were the Mccaffrey's who lived at the far end of the road on the curve on one of the roundabouts. They had two children, one boy and one girl, roughly the same age as me. There were the Morelli's on the opposite side of the roundabout who had two boys slightly older than me. There were also the O'Malley's who lived a little way past the second roundabout. They had two older boys. Then, there were the Petersons who had a boy and a girl of a similar age to me further still from the round-about. It was a great road for playing out, as a car would only come down every hour or so, and with the dog bone layout, there was plenty of racing on bikes. There were also the two school fields where we spent many a day playing cricket and football. Life outside the home was pretty sweet, life inside, not so much.

Although an infrequent visitor, when she was home, one thing I really struggled with was mum's "episodes". Each followed a typical pattern, starting with barely audible mutterings to a low guttural wail that rose until it peaked in shrieks and physical fitting until she passed out on the floor. Once she was quiet, whoever was around would approach cautiously and take out her smelling salts from her blue cardigan pocket and waft them under her nose; she would slowly come around, seemingly oblivious to the preceding drama. It was indeed dramatic, and I remember clearly worrying each time if she would wake up at all. With me being so small and with only a tiny blue bottle to aid me, I remember feeling helpless. I can just about picture her from this time. She was a large woman, quite unrecognisable from the petit beaming bride of 1959. She had jet black hair, flecked with grey and the whitest of skin colours. They met as pen-pals, that quaint pre-digital medium of early long-distance relationships. Dad said it was a toss-up between mum and a previous girlfriend, but he opted for mum because he felt at the time that she would have been easier for him. He has since had to re-evaluate this decision and once even apologised for "not choosing a better mother for us". He was right, if not a little insensitive. Whatever his rationale, it took him quite a while to work out her lack of suitability, and perhaps things may have been different had they stopped with my brothers and stuck with the fashionable 2.4 kids, but I was apparently a "much wished-for girl" - by whom, it's hard to say.

Mum was from Cardiff, the older of two girls. I have a few photographs of her from this time, but nothing that gives any clue as to her personality. As an adult, I asked those who knew her in her earlier years, and the most that they would say was that she was "nice enough". She had no talents anyone thought to mention, no pre-kid ambitions or goals, so I guess you could say that she was unremarkable. In fact, the most remarkable thing she did was die in a mental institution at the age of forty five. The cause of her death was "multiple organ failure". With weekly electric shock treatments, daily multi-dose levels of Valium and an even bigger dose of despair (I can only imagine this part of course), her body just couldn't cope. I remember the big reveal at home. Dad opened the door to our bedroom and quietly announced from the threshold:

"your mother has died". My sister and I just turned over and went to sleep. I was ten years old at the time.

She died in the school summer holidays, so, I was home, but apparently too young to go to the funeral; so I stayed back with a friend of the family to prepare for the wake. It was wonderful to have a woman in the house preparing afternoon tea and I was tasked with cutting up the gingerbread cake. In my excitement, I sliced and arranged it in the shape of a smiley face which may have confused everyone, but I just remember being happy that we were having a party. School routine returned the house to some sort of normality, and I went back to various academic activities. It never occurred to me that I should tell anyone about my mum, so it was with some surprise that towards the end of the first week or so, my teacher took me aside and said how sorry she was. She did this whilst holding me tightly to her chest. I was not sorry at all if my mum's death afforded me such warmth and affection. I imagine I would have stayed held tight to her forever, but she must have pulled away eventually. So, I went back to class as was expected, only to be surrounded by my classmates who were equally affectionate as word got around. To be honest, I was happy with the attention but also baffled as to all the fuss. I realise now, having had my own children, that to lose a mother as a small child is possibly the worst day of anyone's life, but to me, it was not that big a deal. I had hardly known her after all, so I'm sure I didn't quite know what to say.

I have never grieved for my mum, well, not in the usual sense that is. It's hard to grieve for someone you hardly knew, but I felt sorry for her though because she had such a short tragic life. During the later years, I asked myself, did she know what dad was up to? Was she in the hospital voluntarily or was she there to keep her out of the way in some sort of Victorian-style convenience? Or was she driven there by his behaviour? Whatever the truth, I picture a young woman of 25, coming into the marriage all fresh-faced and full of love and optimism, only to die alone just 20 years later. Was it him or was it us? There was nothing much else happening in her life, so it was hard to look elsewhere for answers.

Dad complained bitterly after mum's death, saying that her family had always known of her illness, which he believed had presented itself long before they met. In later years, I met with my mum's sister, and although guarded, it was clear that she had very strong feelings towards my dad and blamed him squarely for what had happened. He had very different views and felt he was tricked into marrying her and that they endorsed the marriage to get her off their hands and into his. I would argue today that it was probably the other way around, but whatever the cause, and by whoever's hand, I didn't question his reasoning. Her random visits were also confusing. Sometimes it was a scheduled visit, but at other times, it was a breakout - a black cab would arrive unannounced and out she'd pop. For the first couple of days, it was nice to have her in the house as she even tried parental duties, but it was always short-lived and rather unsatisfying. I remember vividly her getting up before we left for school one time and attempting breakfast. This was a huge novelty in our house and I sat expectantly wondering what type of meal a mum could produce. To be honest, I should have perhaps just made it myself as I usually did, as the tea was overly sugared, the cereal all mushy and the state she got in to make it was rather disproportionate to the result. I wished I hadn't asked her. I wished even more that she had offered.

Dad always said she was not equipped for daily life and that she loved the hospital. We didn't question his wisdom, but I was always suspicious about this state-ment. I'm sure he loved her in his own way, but that way was sometimes hard to reconcile. He delighted in telling the story more than once, about when he'd come home and she'd eaten the tea that was meant for us kids. To teach her a lesson, he made her eat a full Sara Lee Gateau in one sitting. I can imagine the shame of being force-fed as an ironic attack on her gluttony, and

I equally can't possibly imagine myself doing this to anyone, ever. Dad, however, saw it as a clever idea and would finish the story with a flush of pride as he declared that "she never did it again".

Although her death made no material difference in our house, outside of it was another matter. Aside from the attention at school, neighbours became kinder - there were offers of play dates from school friends' mums and boxes of second-hand toys were left on the doorstep. Playdates were my absolute favourite. One of my earliest school friends invited me to her home where her mum would greet me enthusiastically and we would set about making "sticky toffee fingers" otherwise known as Millionaires Shortbread. Being in a kitchen with a real-life mum was intoxicating. She was so gentle and kind and had the most beautiful soft Irish accent. Once we finished baking, we would watch television in their lounge and have tea, something that was an everyday occurrence for them, but for me, it was magical. I still have mum envy, and I just can't help it. It's because I love their warmth, their softness and their smell. I love the way their eyes soften when they look at their children and I want to be around them all the time. To this day, I have a deep yearning to receive maternal love and I look for it in just about every female relationship. The tens of thousands of hours of love, protection and guidance of a mother is something

I can only imagine. This primal need for maternal love has shaped almost all aspects of my personality, not least my need to care for people in a way I'd like to be cared for. When it comes to love, be it friendships, colleagues, partners or children, the lack of my mum's affection has made me loyal, invested, authentic, loving, generous-spirited and grateful for all that I have. All these aspects of me are real, even if they are tinged with a neediness to be loved; to be valued, to be seen and to be appreciated in return. In life, my need to not be like her drove me to be strong, capable, dependable, resilient, resourceful, and ultimately, by most people's measure, successful. These are the best bits; however, the worst of her loss made me anxious, doubtful, untrusting, cautious, petulant, childish, guarded and easily hurt, particularly if I feel let down by someone I care about. For all outward appearances, I am sensitive to the smallest of slights and can often brood for long periods of time over trivial things. But, I have come to accept all my bad points and have begun tentatively to truly appreciate my good, and yes, the mother I had may have been weak, incapable, absent and unremark-able, but she gave me life and she is one half of me.

This last part is an uncomfortable truth. She was my mum in the factual sense, in that, I was born to her. However, I don't define myself as her daughter because it would imply that she influenced me, guided me, nurtured my talents, healed my hurts, held me when I was scared, led me when I was lost, loved me without judgement, cherished my heart, as well as protected my body and let me know that I was hers and loved above all things. This is the mother I try to be, but as she gave me none of these things, I still struggle to connect with the idea of myself as her daughter.

THE ENIGMA

*D*ad died recently. He had dementia for almost a decade, having lingered way too long, and eventually passed at the age of ninety. They said that he'd hung on way beyond most due to his physical fitness, and dad always kept himself fit. He was teetotal, played tennis until the age of eighty one, had never taken an antibiotic, and due to having not learnt to drive, rode his bike everywhere. Born and raised in India to domiciled Anglo-Indian parents', dad was very much the "bon viveur". He was a talented singer, dancer, tennis and badminton player, and worked for 40 years in the same department of the local council. He was well respected, capable, and resourceful.

I was very proud of him! I would watch his twice-yearly amateur dramatic performances in awe, and although I was not allowed to spend time at the tennis club, I watched him discreetly through the fence. I must say that he was quite a player. He was very proud of us too, and I smiled sweetly as he frequently boasted about his achievement of raising four children single-handedly. I never contradicted him on this as he saw the fact that we had all made it to adulthood as very much the measure of his parenting skills. "What doesn't kill you makes you stronger", he would often say, and he meant it, as we all survived at least.

There were early attempts at taking care of us, but it was limited. Our lack of clothes and food provisions were not exclusively due to the absence of his attention. Dad was living beyond his means. I didn't fully appreciate how bad the financial situation was until I tried to open my own bank account much later, at the age of sixteen, after having left home. I'm not sure if this is still the case, but back then, if anyone in your home or previous home gave any cause for concern to a bank, they would be very wary of you. This rather unfair policy led to my first encounter with a bank manager. Come to think of it, I don't think I've ever met a bank manager since. On the momentous day when I decided to open my first bank account having worked for months for my wealth of £400, I was shocked that Lloyds Bank did not accept my application. In disgust, I marched to NatWest, and again, I was told the same thing. Virtually in tears, as my hard earned cash had taken some time to save (I was earning approximately £1 an hour at the time), I was very upset and went back to Lloyds, as this is where I really wanted to bank. The same very kind manager took me aside and said, "I can't tell you why we cannot accept your money, but I can see that you're upset. All I can say is, just write to this address and enclose £1 and they will send you a credit report." When it arrived, I wasn't entirely sure what to make of it. Although I'd never heard of a 'County Court Judgement', it was explained to me that even one of these financial black marks precluded me from having a bank account. Dad had fifteen of them, one of which was for the supermarket Bejam's, which was closed and knocked down years before.

In this modern age of benefit support, I'm pretty sure that dad would have been entitled to something, however, I don't think it would have occurred to him. Given that he worked for the council, it may have been too close for comfort, and he may not have wanted others to know his personal situation. I also think that he would have been very reluctant to give the impression to anyone that he wasn't coping financially or otherwise. He often told the story of when my mum first started to have short stays at the hospital. According to him, he was assessed over several days by two social workers who wanted to see how he was managing. My dad was a very capable man and convinced these ladies that he was able to change dirty nappies, warm up the bottles and wash and dress his brood. This can't have been easy, as then, nappies were of the Terry variety which were essentially squares of cotton fabric held together with a safety pin. There were no disposable ones. He must have managed alright though, as they duly went away, never to return. I've often wondered what would have happened if they had.

Dad was very sociable. On Mondays it was badminton, Tuesdays and Thursdays included amateur dramatics, Saturdays were kept for tennis and Sundays consisted of various house calls; each event ending in dinner at someone's house. In stark contrast, our food provisions were minimal. Dad would visit the local supermarket on his bike each Saturday morning where he would bring back as much as his budget and bicycle could manage. With two hungry elder brothers, provisions barely lasted into Saturday afternoon, while my sister and I waited patiently to see what slim pickings were left once the boys had had their fill. There were no specific mealtimes as such. Dad tried a few home-made efforts from time to time with his signature dish being deep-fried eggs. This is where you take an egg and drop it straight into a deep saucepan of oil. It is edible for the first three or four uses, post a new oil change, and becomes practically carcinogenic thereafter.

Along with amateur dramatics, tennis and badminton, dad also loved men. As was the predicament of gay men from the 1920s, he could not "come out" as one does in our more tolerant times, but it was not particularly a secret. I first knew when I found his stash of porn magazines under his mattress. The more public displays were evident in his love of male movie stars from the '50s of which he had many posters about his room. It was a room that was technically padlocked, but having inherited much of his resourcefulness, I worked out how to remove the lock hinges and let myself in and out undetected. I don't think I minded about his sexuality, and plus, his porn stash certainly opened my mind.

His men friends came and went, some we got to know, some we didn't. The most significant was a Bostonian actor. He was very handsome and I think dad loved him very much. When he went back to the US, dad followed, leaving us kids to get on with things, much like we always did. He was away for five weeks, leaving his six, seven, ten & thirteen year old children to their own devices.

I swing from dad being my hero to someone who hurt me very deeply. The little girl in me who so desperately needed a strong protector, provider, and guiding hand, had to fend for herself. I did try to get his attention, and would often work hard to find the cracks in which I could fit. He played tennis, and although he never invited me to play, I would learn the game by watching Wimbledon. He loved the theatre, so I would offer to read his lines with him, and if he liked a certain musician, I would learn all their songs. I would do just about anything to connect with him. I also worried about him all the time. When I started to earn my own money, I would spend it on him. For example, I would see to all his bicycle repairs, and when I had enough saved, I would buy him a brand new bike so he would be even safer. I also made sure that it came along with reflective armbands, lights and helmets in the hope that doing so would prevent him from coming to harm. I worried about his comfort and would buy duvets for the winter, and almost his entire wardrobe was bought by me at some point. I also bought all his tennis racquets and gear, but this was more for the joy of pleasing him than for his safety or comfort. This last gesture wasn't entirely for my pleasure; it was also to lessen my shame. Dad smelled bad, really bad. He would never take a bath or wash his clothes, and I was so appalled by this that I would buy him tennis kits as I couldn't bear the idea of him stinking in public. He would accept each gift with genuine pleasure and I would beam with pride at being able to make him happy even though I had none of these things myself. The irony of the carer being cared for by the uncared for, was lost on him.

I guess a therapist would say that I did what I did to take control of the uncontrollable. I only had one parent, and absent as he was, I didn't want to lose him too. But, I also think I bought him things just so he would like me, and more importantly, notice me. We didn't talk as such, and I have very few memories of fatherly advice. The only ones I recall are, 'wash your face and hands', 'never kiss in public' and 'always be polite'. We had a crude but effective system of communication. I would write a note of the things I needed him to buy for me and slip it under his door, and he would duly act on the request. Puberty was something I had to learn for myself, and the first time I bled, it was very Carrie-esq, except it was not in the shower but in the middle of a classroom. With no one to ask about such things and it being my pre-earning days, I had to find a method to get what I needed. So, every month, I would let him know what sanitary towels I required by leaving a note under his door. Without a word, he would place them discreetly in a drawer in my bedroom the next day. Even now, I hate buying period products, such is my hard-wired embarrassment.

In addition to keeping him safe with cycling safety equipment, I worried about him getting AIDS. When I first discovered his sexuality, it was the early 1980's and the fear of AIDS was rife. I couldn't talk to him directly about it, nor my friends, so this anxiety could only be expressed in my version of prayers. As I looked up to the stars, I would bargain with the universe; saying, "I would be good and kind and do my best so long as you keep him safe." Such was my anxiety that I would wait up until the early hours just to hear him wheel his bike down the side of the house, and only then would I relax enough to go to sleep.

To most kids at this time, being good would mean doing their homework, cleaning their teeth, and generally doing as they were told. These rules were typically set by a parent or guardian and would have consequences and possibly rewards associated with them. I look at my own children and wonder how many days it would take them to go feral if I didn't constantly remind them to do all these things. In my case, with no mum and an absent dad, my teeth were never brushed and school was optional, so being good meant something very different to me. Being good was about survival as it directly related to accessing essentials like food and clothing. For example, I worked out that if I alphabetised my friend's dad's video collection, he would let me visit more often for tea with his daughter, if I made one good bike out of three broken ones, my friend would keep me around longer, if I offered to watch over the pool whilst the lifeguard's sunbathed, they would let me come in for free and I could stay all day, and if I washed and dried all the leisure centre towels, they would give me free lunches and I could also wash my clothes. This was what being good meant to me and it worked well.

I also learned very early to look after myself in other ways. When other kids hurt themselves, I imagine they would run to a parent or guardian, who would, in turn, do their best to help, and if further medical support was needed, it would be sought out. For me, it was a case of working it out for myself. One such example was the day I dropped a large glass mirror directly onto my big toe. It had long lost its frame, so it was just a heavy piece of glass that I had dropped onto my bare feet from about a metre high. When it struck, the pain was so intense that I felt the air from my body leave me and I wasn't even able to scream out. I just fell to the floor in shock. When I could finally look to see what I had done, my big toe was a mess. The glass had hit it square across the toenail bed and it had started to swell. It was also at a funny angle, so, my instinct was to grab it and hold it back to where it should have been. I then looked around for something to keep it straight and found masking tape. Thankfully, it stopped bleeding quite quickly, so the tape did the job of at least holding it in place. The last piece of resourcefulness needed was how I would be able to walk after this. My toe was so badly swollen that shoes were not possible. However, I had a pair of white school plimsolls and just cut the end off to allow my swollen toe to peak out. Over time, the nail came off and the toe eventually healed as best it could. It still causes me pain to this day, as the bone was indeed broken and perhaps would have benefited from being set properly. Dog bites, bike crashes, tree falls and burns were all self-treated. So yes dad, I agree that what doesn't kill you really does make you stronger, at least on the outside.

Having survived to sixteen, I determined I was ready to leave and make my own way. Being absent most of the time, it was some weeks before my dad noticed, which I would laugh about at the time. It was much later that I began to question him. His view of our childhood was very different from our reality. I often wondered about this; how could he not have seen how we lived? Why did he not take care of us? Why did he not stop my brother? I still can't be sure. One theory is that dad was overindulged as a child and lacked empathy as well as basic caring instincts and ability. Another idea is that it was he who had a mental illness and mum was quite well but just died of sadness. He certainly was an enigma. During my adult years, even though we lived in the same town, he stayed an ethereal presence, occupying no more than the position of a genial gent that I would see in the street now and then. If we did bump into each other, he was always pleased to see me and would enquire about my work, friends, and travel plans and we'd generally chit-chat for a short while before going our separate ways. He was often in town on his bicycle, and to this day, if I catch sight of an old man on a bike, my heart lifts just a little as it used to back then; so desperate was I to see him.

GRANNY AND SONS

*G*randad died of lung cancer just one month after my mum, so dad decided that granny should move in with us. To the outsider, this would have been a perfectly sensible arrangement - a surrogate mum for us and maybe someone to keep house. However, the reality was far different.

Born and raised in India, with all the trappings of being British at the time of the Raj, she never really recovered from the shock of having to leave her home country. In her prime, she was a ward sister for a state hospital in Mumbai. I have a photo of her looking very grand in her full nurse regalia, and I know she was very proud of her work there. She lived in Colaba, just a stone's throw from the famous Taj Hotel, and one of the more prestigious parts of the city - a far cry from the cramped one-bedroomed flat in England which was all she could afford once Partition had led to India not being safe for Anglo Indians. Prior to leaving her birthplace, she enjoyed bearers, servants, housekeepers, and nannies. Dad said that they had seven staff members in total, one for almost every task, including making her daily G&T. According to a much-enjoyed impression by my dad, she would shout, "Bear-rah!", at the top of her voice, and he would dutifully run to her side and pass it to her from the table in front of her as it was just slightly out of reach. She loved parties, tennis clubs, dances and all the culinary delights of India. Although safer, moving to the UK must have felt like all the light and colour of her life had gone out forever. Her home in England was tiny, and like many refugees coming down in the world, it was stuffed with way too many possessions from their previous, grander lives. It was not a happy home as she and my grandad argued constantly. The resentment simmered menacingly in the air between them, neither happy at how the second half of their lives had panned out.

My dad was born in Mumbai in 1929. He was the eldest of three sons and absolutely loved his time in India. He had his fair share of challenges - there was the time his dogs had to be shot due to rabies and his best friend lost his leg under a truck playing a game of 'who can leave their leg in the road the longest', as the truck with no tyres came along. This being pre-antibiotic days, dad had to survive with nothing but Beechams powders and iodine against whatever India could throw at him, including Malaria and the whole gamut of childhood diseases. But he loved it all the same, and when you see pictures of him during these times, he is so full of vitality and always surrounded by many friends.

As a young man, he was of slim build and slightly effete. He had a wisp of a moustache and early balding led to a precarious comb-over. Well-heeled and fancy-free, he enjoyed all the same trappings as his parents. Life was sweet but it was time to go, and the whole family packed up and left for England on the HMS Batory in 1952, never to return.

Once settled in England, the family lived together for a short time, but as time moved on, they each went their separate ways. The middle brother lived and worked about five miles from us, a fact I only discovered in my twenties, having never met him in my childhood, as he and my dad had fallen out. They reconciled tragically at the funeral of their youngest brother who had died of AIDS, aged fifty nine. They cried for their fraternal loss but wept even more for the wasted twenty eight years of time since they'd last seen each other, neither remembering nor choosing to bring up what they had fallen out over. They became close in their final years, which I was glad about, even if I found my new uncle to be a rather melancholy, bitter man. As for their tragic little brother, he made periodic appearances during my childhood. He was an actor, artist, and professional ballet dancer. In his prime, he shared the same stage as Nureyev, and it was rumoured that he also shared the bed of a famous leading film actor who is still "in the closet". With his own film-star good looks, blonde hair, piercing blue eyes and extraordinary physique, my uncle would have been quite the catch. Even today, I boast about him and have often entertained the idea in jest that I was his love child. Like him, I have fair hair and olive skin, whereas my siblings have dark-hair and are fair skinned. Before he took up his more creative side, he was also a sailor. I have a photo of him on one of his ships and he looks so happy; a far cry from his final days where he died alone in his foetid flat, discovered some weeks later by neighbours offended by the smell of decaying flesh.

Granny's arrival initially looked quite promising to us kids and it was a boon to dad, as with a woman in the house, this allowed him to fly the nest even more than he'd already self-bargained, to be reasonable. This would have been an excellent plan except, a) she hated us - dad was the apple of her eye and the fact that he had saddled himself with a large brood was very inconvenient, and b) she had what we understood to be early-stage dementia and hallucinated most of the time. Unfortunately, the voices in her head were not keen on us either. The only improvement being, that with his share of her flat sale, dad invested in a loft conversion and created two small bedrooms. It was good news for us girls as we now had a proper mould-free room.

At under five ft, it's hard to imagine why I was so scared of her, but she was so angry all the time, even before dementia rendered her, well...demented. She would prowl around the house in her synthetic night-ies, shouting, "You fucking bastard woman - you stole my Ernie." Ernie being her late husband, and the woman in question, Sheila Crickleshank, who as far as I knew was a fictional character of her own making. Pots, pans, wooden spoons and whatever was at hand would be used to hit us with and accentuate every sylla-ble. Most of her rantings were harmless and barely registered with me. She became just another bit-part player in my already chaotic life. There were certain things that were mortifying though, such as the time I had to go to the post office with a coat, as she was completely naked telling everyone that she was the Queen of England. She also had a habit of sitting in the nude by her bedroom window, again, waiting for her carriage to take her to Sandringham. I can laugh at these memories now, but as a teenage girl trying to fit in, it was extremely embarrassing, and I think I might have hated her in certain moments.

She died, aged eighty. Not a bad innings as she outlived her husband by 10 years. Breast cancer was what finally got her, but not until the very end. It was discovered only by chance. Granny was a hoarder and as her dementia progressed, her raging increased and she was best avoided. The house itself was none too fragrant, so it took quite a lot to break through with something specific, but for about a week, there was a particularly rancid sour smell coming from her room. Once or twice when she prised open the door, my dad and I would sneak in and look around to see what was causing such a foul stench. It smelt like rotting flesh, so we assumed she had left some meat to go off and hadn't noticed its decay. But, apart from the usual smell of urine and stale sweat, we couldn't find anything that could produce something of such potency. Frustrated, my dad finally decided to force the door open while she was inside and catch in the act whatever she was hiding in there. She was indeed hiding something, a gaping wound stretched across her left breast. Seeping with gangrenous matter, the smell was indeed rotting flesh, but not of a discarded chicken breast as we'd thought, but her own. She had been treating a 12-inch tumour with just iodine and self-belief.

The local GP was called, and once she'd realised that

the game was up, it was like Mr. Hyde had fled to leave Dr. Jekyll surrendered to his fate. The raging, incessant rantings all stopped in that instant as she handed herself over to the much-feared medical professional. Although a ward sister herself, or maybe because of this, she always said, "keep away from those hospitals." But, with an open wound that the GP felt was at least a decade old, she had no choice but to go quietly.

Post-surgery, she was able to come home. Weakened, and virtually bed-bound, she relied on her meals and drinks being brought to her. I had left home at this stage and worked about three miles away. So, I would cycle home during my lunch break to make her favourite - boil-in-the-bag parsley, peas and mashed potatoes. I also carried her to the bathroom and wiped her bottom and "penny" as she called it. This may sound heroic, but she was light as a feather. I carried her with such care, careful not to bruise her, as she had almost no meat on her bones and her skin was as thin and mottled as crepe paper. I did this most days, sometimes riding over after work too, to make her a cup of tea. My eldest brother would often be in the next room, but he hated granny and didn't want to be a hypocrite, so refused to help. I, on the other hand, didn't mind at all. In those last few weeks, I learnt much about her life. Her dementia gone, she talked endlessly about her sisters, her time in India, how she'd lost her father in the first world war and many stories related to her home country. The doctors said that they didn't believe she had dementia at all as her mind had been affected by cancer, and its toxic presence in her body caused inflammation and fever. Once it had been cut out, her demons were released. She spent her last weeks in the local hospital. Again, I would cycle there after work, either with my dad or, I would meet him there and we would talk until she was tired. I can't prove it, but I think the doctors helped her on her way as I noticed that the saline drip had been removed and no food was offered. She died just a few days afterwards. If true, it was an unspoken kindness, and I am grateful to the person brave enough to make this decision and ease her suffering.

Her funeral was a sad affair. This once gregarious bon viveur, this pocket-rocket tennis-loving tyrant who brought the party to life in her prime and served the country of her birth with pride in its hospital wings, was laid to rest with just my dad, my sister and our newly reconciled uncle. My eldest brother, still clinging to his principles, refused to attend, and my other brother was not well enough. In her heyday, she probably imagined a mass of people celebrating her colourful life, but it seems that her circle of friends shrunk as she did, and in the end, it was just the four of us. Despite her darker shadows, I loved her. She was strong, resilient, driven, and purposeful, and in certain lights, I like to think we were alike. I have her eyes for example - she always had a kind of knowing in them, a conspiratorial crinkle at the edges, challenging you to take life on as she had done.

THE BROOD

My siblings and I are, amazingly, still in each other's lives. Barely a week goes by without some form of contact, and when we meet up there's very little room for anyone else as we boisterously bicker and tease as siblings usually do. There's honesty between us, a bond of shared experience, and despite our differences, there's no ego and almost nothing we won't say to each other. I find this a small miracle given the extreme nature of our past encounters.

My eldest brother is very much the patriarch. Six years older than me, he was sixteen when mum died, and with dad absent, it was naturally assumed that he would take up the responsibility, and has continued in his role to this day. Tall and athletic with jet-black hair and fair skin, he's a keen goalkeeper and has played for the same club for 25 years. He has his own business which he takes enormous pride in and is as enthusiastic about it today as he was when he first set it up over 30 years ago. He has loved and been loved by his wife of 32 years and has lived in *"Dogbone St."* for over 40 years. My big brother has the same hairdresser, dentist, doctor, and loyal set of friends from childhood, and even has the same trainers. Not the same pair of course, but each year he will buy a set of green and white Hi-Tec squash shoes, a brand he discovered in the '80s and hasn't felt the need to try any other one since then. You could say he's a man who doesn't like change! I link this need for stability to his need for control, not in a threatening way as he can be playful and silly when in the company of others, but if you get him on his own, he's brooding and serious, something very few people get to see as he's intensely private. We have on occasion talked about our childhood. He was guarded at first, but as we talked, he opened up more and more. He stops shy of open criticism of dad but will at least acknowledge his shortcomings, so, I understand his loyalty. Dad may have been lacking in many ways but he and my brother lived together for many years, and although complex, their bond was strong. It's not that he never left home as he is no "Timothy Lumsden", but it was more that our father's home became his. When dad retired at sixty five, he wasn't able to make the final payment on his mortgage, so he did a deal. In return for signing over the house for the value of the remaining debt, dad would be allowed to live rent-free in the house until the end of his days. This may be considered a sweet deal, but the intervening 25 years before my father finally died in his bedroom were not easy on my brother. Like the deal stuck with the devil at the crossroads, it brought him some benefits but at a heavy cost to his liberty.

Although we are very close now, for many years things were strained. For most of his adult life, he felt guilty about not protecting me. To be fair, the worst of my experiences happened whilst he was away, so the guilt he feels is a little misplaced. As a grown man, looking back, he feels that he could have done more. But I have never felt badly towards him. He had to deal with things his own way, which mostly manifested in him being absent, and albeit, for different reasons, he had his own challenges. He's popular and affable now but he was an angry young man, and in particular, found dad's sexuality very difficult to manage. When he discovered dad's porn stash about the same time as I did, where I was curious, he was enraged. He put all the magazines in black plastic bags, wheeled them to the local dump and set fire to the lot. I also recall him begging our father not to go to Boston. It wasn't the fact that he was leaving us for weeks on end, it was that he was going with a man. Although not homophobic, it's a very different matter when you're a teenage boy making your own way, and if he had idealistic visions of a masculine patriarch who came to watch his football matches, went to the pub, helped with his car maintenance and any other imagined father/son bonding, his actual dad fell very short of this ideal. Whatever his reasons, he wasn't best pleased, and coupled with our chaotic home situation, he dealt with it by spending long periods of time with his friends; anything to be out of the house. When he was home, he was a simmering bag of rage, seething with frustration at how life had turned out, and so, was not at all good to be around for much of the time. I caught the wrong side of him a few times. These skirmishes were more hurtful emotionally than physically, as I genuinely wanted to please him, and like a dutiful dog, I would skulk away from my master, wondering what I had done to offend him. I may have been on his wrong side from time to time, but mostly, he vented his rage on his younger brother, not without good reason.

As well as all his hobbies and sports, my eldest brother loves cars. He currently has three vintage Jaguars and polishes them each weekend to a high shine, then takes each one out, in turn for a drive. His first ever car was a Ford Cortina which he bought with his own savings at age 18. It was electric blue with chrome bumpers and was literally the love of his life. You can imagine his rage when he woke up one morning to find it missing. My younger brother had taken it out for a spin and only made it to the next street before he crashed it into a fence. Rather than confess, he left it there and ran away. Dad, in a rare moment of intervention, begged his eldest son not to kill his little brother, and so, he was spared the thrashing of his life.

As a child, my middle brother was what my dad would have referred to as a "lump". He was a big baby, a big toddler, a big kid, a big adolescent and is now a big middle-aged man. I was three years younger and a skinny little thing throughout my childhood, and therefore, at some considerable physical disadvantage which was unfortunate given his obsession with me. When I was six, for example, he dragged me over a folded mattress which flung open and tore one side of my face to shreds. I must have looked terrible as dad was asked to come into school to explain what had happened. Another time, he waited in the bushes and shoved a stick through the spoke of my bike wheel which sent me flying and scraped up my face badly, yet again. This time though, he was spotted in the act by a neighbour and she gave him a real telling off. There was the classic sit on my chest and drop 'loogies' into my face antics, smearing peanut butter in my mouth and nose as he knew it made me feel sick, along with farting in my face while sitting on the reverse of my chest. I'm sure every little girl who has an older brother can relate to some, if not all, of the above; however, he was not a regular older brother, which began to manifest and become clearer as he hit his early teens.

As he grew, so did his inventiveness. He could devise pain from almost every instrument and every situation. He knew I loved my dog for example. She was a stray whom dad took in when I was around eight years old. No lover of animals, my brute of a brother worked out that if he enraged her enough, she would go to attack him - more out of panic than aggression - and as she did so, with precision accuracy he would slam her face into the doorframe, laughing psychotically as she recoiled from the blow. For him, it was a double victory, as distressing my dog also distressed me. I recall vividly the impotent rage I had at the injustice of his behaviour, and my own self-loathing for not being strong enough to fight him back. But, how could I fight back? I was tiny compared to him and before long, my once contented loyal pet became a nervous wreck and had an "unexplained" heart attack at the age of four.

I use the word psychotic purposefully because as he went from boy to adolescent, the true extent of his violence peaked. "Violent Paranoid Schizophrenia" was the eventual diagnosis, but not for many years. Prior to this discovery, my sister and I were left to fend for ourselves with this brooding stalking mass of extreme chemical imbalance. The closest depiction that resembles just what it was like to share a home with him was the brilliant James McAvoy's portrayal of a schizophrenic in the film, Split. My brother didn't share the multiple personalities that occupied McAvoy's head but the intensity and speed in which the character he portrayed would shift from passivity to full-on maniac was extremely resonant for me. The way my brother moved was animalistic. Prowling, sniffing and sensing his world rather than cognitively evaluating it. He gave off a sour smell, a pungent rancid odour, caused by not eating anything other than white bread, which he would chew and then spit out all over the house. He would shift from catatonic to manic in seconds, and you had to be alert in both instances. I took to virtually running past him when he was in the house, just in case he caught me by the arm and pulled me into whatever dark reality was playing in his mind at that exact moment. Completely unprotected and being the main outlet for his rage, this episode of his life was life-altering for me.

I carry numerous scars from his physical attacks. I have an eight-inch scar on my back from when he slashed across it with a ballpoint pen. I had my back to him as I was washing up and the first I knew he was even in the room was when I felt a thump on it. At first, I thought he had just punched me, but as the initial shock subsided, the searing pain of the cut began to appear. There was no warning, no preface, just something in his mind that urged him to grab whatever was on hand and attack me. I also have a diamond-shaped scar where he plunged the shard of a broken plate deep into my forearm, and a similarly shaped scar, albeit smaller, just above my eyelid, where he opened a window onto my face as I ran along the back of the house. There was one incident that although produced no lasting scar, I'll never forget.

In one of his random attacks, I remember that I started at the top of the stairs, but in a second, I was at the bottom, being pulled by my hair along the floor. He beat me with whatever was at hand, this time being a melamine old-style click-and-whirr phone and a bar of soap. He beat me repeatedly in a blaze of rabid force until he exhausted himself. This time, I had a witness, albeit a helpless one in the form of my younger sister. She begged me to stay down, but I was so enraged by the injustice of him being nothing more than just bigger than me, after each manic wave of blows, I would stagger to my feet and meet his eye. This, of course, only made him even more determined to hurt me, but I wouldn't back down. Eventually, he slinked away and I could assess the damage. I was battered and bruised with a few cuts, but nothing that wouldn't heal with time. Even if I could seek help, I had no one to go to, so, I just dusted myself off and went to my bedroom, not telling anyone, as I reasoned that it would only make things worse.

The physical scars hurt at the time but the psychological scars went much deeper. Daytimes were dangerous, and as his illness progressed, I had to find strategies to avoid his manic outbursts which I mostly managed, but at night I had very little protection; not even a bedroom door which he had long smashed to bits in one of his rages. Sleep was a calculated choice. It was either that I stayed awake and listened to his mutterings about all the things he was going to do to me, or, fall asleep and succumb to his demonic imaginings. I was a coiled spring of tension, ever ready for the expected yet unpredictable timings of attack. I still don't sleep well and I'm very sensitive to aggression, and will therefore work hard to not provoke negative emotions in others. This, I realise, is at the expense of asserting my own feelings, often backing off from a verbal fight in case it escalates. It's a complex thing to explain but its essence is that it is better to keep the peace rather than risk experiencing your perceived insignificance and consequent impotence against a stronger physical force. Rather like a lion batting away at a mouse; the mouse may have much to offer, but to the physical mass of the lion, it is nothing.

He was sectioned, eventually. The police arrested him, not for his abuse of me, which of course they knew nothing about, but for throwing stones at cars. I breathed a sigh of relief as I thought it was the beginning of the end of his threat to me, but it was short-lived. My eldest brother went to the hospital and managed to convince them that he could take care of him and that he would be better off at home. I guess having seen the effects of institutionalised care on our mother, he was confident of this decision. This may have been a good decision, but for me, not so much.

Amazingly, I'm still in his life. I forgave my middle brother for the worst of his abuses as he was so deeply in his psychosis that he doesn't remember much of what happened. The childhood tantrums that I wrote about earlier were the beginning of expressions of his undiagnosed condition, and with no parents around to intervene, he was left to express himself without boundaries. If you met him now, you'd find him talkative and nice enough, if a little "off", in that, he doesn't listen and only talks about himself, at great length and tempo. His nickname is "Ariston", as he literally goes on and on. Amazingly, he has only had one other psychotic episode in his adult years and has maintained a long-standing marriage. His wife has advanced

Multiple Sclerosis and it's very touching to watch this once, sometimes violent man, so careful and considerate of her needs. Another reason for my forgiveness toward him is that I was not entirely an angel. I may not have had the strength to hurt him physically but I had a quick mind and used this to hurt him emotionally. When my rage at his brute strength against my physical weakness peaked, I thought of the worst thing I could say and went straight for his weak spot - his sexuality. As far as I know, he is straight, but that didn't matter. The fact is, he didn't like the idea of being thought of as gay, maybe because he also had issues with his dad's preferences too, so I would take my revenge by saying that he was. I'm ashamed to say that I used every derivative slang word I could come up with and roped my little sister into the enterprise. I feel terrible about this now, as I'd heard from a family friend recently that it had really distressed him. Unbeknownst to me at the time, he was bullied terribly at school, and along with his big brother taking lumps out of him, it might explain his need to unleash his pain onto his smaller, weaker sibling. I'm proud to say that the buck stopped with me. I absorbed all his punches and somehow managed to protect my little sister from physical harm; like some unspoken sororal pact that I was the stronger one, both physically and emotionally, and therefore had to stand between them.

Then lastly, there's my little sister. Born just 16 months after me, she was greeted with even more indifference from our mother than my own inauspicious arrival, and I often wonder about how she came to be. Mum was clinically depressed when I was born, so quite how she was up for trying for another just a few short months after my arrival, is baffling.

She looks like my mum. Dark-haired, fair-skinned, as well as a physical resemblance, and then there's the shared lack of capacity to deal with life. Whether this is nature or nurture is a question worth considering. We grew up together in the same various bedrooms and share, at least, some of both parents' DNA. But, whatever the combination of factors, or maybe just plain old bad luck, she was not dealt the best set of cards. As a child, she had a happy-go-lucky disposition, born from low intelligence rather than legitimate joyfulness. To this day, she has little recall of the darker elements of her childhood. Her simplified view of the world glosses over the awfulness of it all and she holds onto the smallest of good memories, retelling them repeatedly, as if she were constructing her own version of reality. In her eyes, dad could do no wrong and I have so far not corrected her as I've reasoned that it's more important to preserve her distorted memory than it is for me to put the record straight. To me, her Stockholm-Syndrome-Esq relationship with him so obviously betrays her need to be loved. I find this intriguing, given the volume of evidence against him. She lost eight teeth by the time she was in her twenties, is barely literate, and has the emotional regulation of a toddler. She can swing from outward cheerfulness to the blackest spitting rage almost in an instant, and each of us has experienced our fair share of her uncontrolled tantrums. She has never worked, save for a few part-time short-lived shop roles, and is a constant worry to us all. We forgive even the most extreme behaviours as we all recognise that she is by far the most damaged from our childhood neglect.

In her teenage years, boyfriends came and went, and I rarely got to meet them. Several short-lived skir-mishes later, I noticed she was putting on a little weight. She laughed and said that she'd been eating more than usual and I didn't think very hard about it. As the weeks went by, I began to suspect it was more than extra pudding that was causing her shape to change. She continued to reject this idea, and when I asked her when her last period was, she said it was several months ago but not to worry as it was just her hormones playing up. In any case, I didn't have to wait long for my suspicions to be confirmed. She called me on the phone, and between each hysterical sob, explained that she'd been to the doctors, and yes, she was indeed pregnant - 23 weeks along, in fact. With the father long gone, we all braced ourselves for the gift and likely challenge of her forthcoming child.

Three days past her due date, she called me at work to say that she was having an allergic reaction as blood was coming out of her. I was CEO of the Academy of Contemporary Music at the time. Famed for hosting, albeit briefly, Ed Sheeran, it was widely considered a world-leading music industry institute. I joined ACM in my early thirties, initially part-time as it suited me to be more local as I had two young children. I knew the owner through a mutual friend and we hit it off straight away. I joined initially to connect the institute to the music industry by way of creating a department that focussed entirely on creating commercial opportunities for the students. This was radical in 2004 and although universities now are very much industry engaged, ACM was awarded a Queen's Award for Innovation in 2008 for pioneering this approach. Although Ed was by far my most high-profile student, we had many more industry successes during my time, including Newton Faulkner, Ted Dwane from Mumford and Sons, Zomboy and many more to note. One closest to my heart was our Gospel Choir. They were doing extremely well in the BBC competition, Last Choir Standing, and the BBC film crew were in filming rehearsals and back-story interviews. So, when my sister called to say she had an allergic reaction, it was not a good time to be dealing with her hysterical call, but I listened patiently. Having worked out what was really going on, I explained that it was highly unlikely that a new body lotion was going to cause this and that she should meet me at the hospital.

I found her in the car park, pacing and still in complete denial of what was happening. I explained calmly that her baby was coming and that the car park was no place to bring a child into the world. Once she was inside the maternity ward and settled into a room, I spoke to the team and suggested they plan for a caesarean, as, in my opinion, her participation in a natural birth was very unrealistic. I had previously birthed two children myself and knew what was coming, and to me anyway, it was obvious that my sister was not going to take part. They thanked me politely for my guidance and proceeded to ignore me completely and try everything to have her deliver naturally. Several distressing hours later, with everything from uncontrollable wailing to complete disengagement, as predicted, they prepped her (and me) for a caesarean. I was relieved to meet the surgeon and anaesthetist, and was looking forward to taking part in the miracle of modern obstetrics, but they took one look at my sister and decided that a routine caesarean was not possible and I was asked to leave as they prepared her for general anaesthesia. They explained to me afterwards that within seconds of seeing the emotional state she was in, there was a real risk of her attempting to leave the table during the procedure, hence the decision to put her fully under. Thirty minutes later, her daughter was handed to me whilst her mum was stitched and rested in the recovery room.

Motherhood turned out to be a mixed bag. On the one hand, it was a blessing - a new member of the family came into our lives, and miraculously, my sister settled down with a very loyal and steady good man who has done his best to raise her daughter as his own. On the other, it requires constant vigilance from the rest of us; family, friends, teachers, social workers, and health professionals have all kept things as steady as possible, and we are praying that as my niece grows, all her collective surrogate parents will be able to guide her safely through to adulthood.

I'm a little ashamed to admit that my sister idolises me. I love her too, but I'm not a very good sister to her. We have never sat together in a restaurant or gone to a bar, cinema, or shop, as I find being in her company extremely difficult. I wish I could accept her as she is, but she reminds me too much of my mum. I also think I reject her as I suspect she is the darkest side of myself. I look at her and see my childish petulant self, my needy, wanting, unreasonable self. She is the shadow that I won't let out. For me, it's better to keep my distance than be confronted with that uncomfortable truth. I also believe that for me to be there for the bigger issues of her life, I have to keep away from the day-to-day, as what she would class as normal, affects me for a long time. For this reason, it is safer for me to create a natural boundary.

So, that's us, the fab four, and despite our differences, I love them all! They are the people I have known the longest, and the shared memory of our childhood, although each of us had a very different experience, keeps us bonded. Adults at the time may have considered intervening and handing us over to social care. We may have led alternate, possibly better childhood years, but it would most likely have meant that we would have been split up. Dad hurt us in many ways, but even if it was for selfish reasons, he kept us all together, which is something that I'm very grateful for. When my sister married, spontaneously and unselfconsciously, the four of us took to the dance floor, and with our arms around each other, we danced with abandon, despite everything we had seen, inflicted and endured, somehow our love for each other prevails. Dad watched from the side-lines, his dementia had prevented him from his usual fancy footwork, but I'd like to think that at that moment, some small part of his brain flickered and he felt super proud of his brood.

ELLIE

I first set eyes on Ellie when I was seven years old, and it was love at first sight. She was in her thirties when we first met. Tall, tanned, confident and purposeful, I knew who she was by her dad's description of her. Her father lived opposite me in *Dogbone St.* and was very proud of his youngest daughter, as he boasted her achievements endlessly to me. I was too young to understand that living in Knightsbridge and working in Mayfair were two very big achievements, but with her strawberry blonde hair, gorgeous freckles, and unselfconscious laugh, I didn't care what she did for a living, I just needed to know her. At first, I would just sidle up to her on one of my many visits to her dad's. He was a lovely man, that quintessential Englishman of his time; patient, kind, generous, completely comfortable in his own skin and with the contentment of a life well lived. He would spend hours teaching me the secrets of a great vegetable garden or how to work a piece of wood gripped into a vice, attached to his worn workbench. I loved how the metal handle spun with just a flick of my tiny little finger until it required his strong hands to lock it into place. He asked no questions of me, preferring to accept this new little life into his, and I would spend hours doing whatever he was doing, be it watching daytime TV next to his open fire or pottering around his garden which was full of curiosities.

Ellie would visit most weekends and I would ache to see her. I would give her a little while to settle in, then run across the road and reach up to the doorbell on my tippy toes. Her dad would usually answer, and I would run under his arm, into the lounge and launch into telling Ellie absolutely everything that had occurred in the long week since I'd last seen her. I would do this whilst she carried on with her chores and just follow her around, much like the hoover she was dragging behind her, snaking to her every movement. One of my favourite things to do was watch her unpack in her bedroom. Her weekend bag was full of bottles and creams, and she would place each carefully on the white-wooden dresser which was set against a backdrop of various subtle shades of pink. I would crinkle my toes on her carpet and bounce up and down expectantly, to see what else would appear from her case. Against the dankness of my own home with all its distortions of masculinity, this was paradise – a real-life womanly woman – capable, funny, warm, and affectionate, and for the weekend at least, mostly mine. She had inherited her dad's patience and would spend hours explaining things to me, from the simple reason for brushing one's teeth to the more obscure need to not eat chocolate in the back of her car "in case a bride sits in the back and her dress may be ruined". I learnt that tight jeans would give me thrush and that I had to wash my hands after each visit to the loo, otherwise, I might as well "lick the toilet seat". Most important of all, I experienced the intoxicating, addictive nature of making her laugh.

Today, I consider myself, if not laugh-out-loud funny, then at least humorous, which all started with Ellie. Making her laugh was my single biggest joy. Her dad's small bungalow had a curtain sectioning off a lean-to, which made for the perfect backstage preparation space. Once ready, Ellie would announce in her loud confident voice that I was about to take the stage, and out I would come, swishing back the curtains in a melodramatic flourish as my act would begin. Joke telling, mimicry, storytelling or just plain goofing around, I would put on a show with one clear agenda, to see her laugh. And boy could she laugh! A full-throated, head-backed true laugh-out-loud experience it was. I would finish my show with more over-acting, and to much applause from my captive and rather partisan audience. My need to make her happy didn't stop with entertaining, I painted for her, wrote poems for her and just about everything I did was tinged with the imaginings of just how proud I would make her feel with the results. I'm not sure quite how she introduced herself, but she would attend parents' evenings and enquire as to my progress, as I sat proudly, basking in her magnificence.

Her interest in my education lasted way into my secondary school. She felt I had the intelligence to go into law and was keen that I pursued a profession. Her absolute ambition for me was that I become a barrister. I wanted to please her, and for a time I applied myself as best I could, but with homelife becoming more and more chaotic, I found other non-academic distractions and her interest waned, which I took more as a let-off than a lack of care in my future. It was some time before I realised that she was distracted. While I was in my late teens, she was diagnosed with breast cancer.

She announced it with typical Ellie bravado. It was something to be beaten and she was rising to the challenge. Given that she had just personally finished building a two-storey extension to her new home, I didn't doubt her ability to master this new situation. Everything about Ellie was exceptional. She travelled between Perth and London as a commercial liaison for Australia House. On the weekdays, she wore Chanel suits and lived in Knightsbridge. During the weekends, she donned hobnail boots and renovated a riverside house she had bought to be near her dad in his advancing years. In addition to her career, her construction skills and dedication to her father, she was a wonderful artist, jewellery maker and musician. Her home was full of extensions of her personality, with imprints of her creativity almost everywhere. I particularly liked her jewellery making which focused on the polishing of rough-hewn opal stones brought back from her beloved Australia. Her range of skills were astounding, so I had no doubt at all that she would take the diagnosis in her stride.

Throughout her treatment, she would talk little of her own suffering and focus only on my news. I would update her on all my latest comings and goings, completely ignoring the physical signs of her illness that were displayed right in front of me. Early chemotherapy thinned her once-lustrous strawberry blonde hair, and her once athletic, hod carrying strength of a body weakened, rendering her breathless with even the smallest of actions. I would do my best to carry on as normal, seeking every opportunity to make her laugh, impress her or distract her in any way I could. Her sense of humour carried her in the early stages. I remember blushing wildly, as the night before her double mastectomy, she whipped off her t-shirt, followed by her sizeable bra, and announced, "Take a good look ladies, this is the last time you can enjoy the sight of these babies!", to a room full of all her close girlfriends. The mood was high, but even I could tell that their hearts were breaking for their dear, brave friend.

The surgery went well. She'd decided to not bother with reconstruction, which I interpreted more an expression of her feminist views than a resignation to her fate. Over the coming months, wave after wave of chemotherapy took her to the very edge of her willpower, and just when I thought I couldn't bear to see her go through anything more, she announced that the cancer had gone into remission. The relief was like breaking the surface of water and taking that first, desperate breath, just in the nick of time. Great sobs of joy belched from my body as she pulled me into her. She'd done it! My beautiful, talented Ellie had beaten her illness, and all would be well.

Post her illness, my life took multiple twists and turns, and Ellie became, as most "parents" do, background noise to my exciting new adult life. I would call her often, but in-person visits became less frequent. It wasn't just my new freedoms; she had a new man in her life too. He was a bookish, awkward, cantankerous man, and where other men had come and gone, this one had moved in. To this day, I couldn't say if they were lovers. I hope not, as if they were, she had punched below her weight, as earlier boyfriends had met a much higher standard, in my opinion. As he was always there, and as keen on me as I was on him, which is to say not at all, my visits became almost non-existent. It was sometime later that we sat in her summer house overlooking the water when she told me the cancer had returned, and that this time, there was nothing they could do. She was just fifty nine at the time and I was now in my mid-twenties. I cursed the time wasted in the intervening years. How could I have been so complacent! How could I not have thought that every moment of her life on this planet was a bonus, and that my future with her in it was not promised, with each year sacrosanct. The air I had once breathed in with such relief left me like a sucker punch. Everything in that moment came into focus as I stared intently back at her and dismissed her words. "They don't know that! Anything could happen from here!" I shouted. The strength of my denial only making things worse, but I didn't care. This was my Ellie, and if she couldn't fight anymore, then I would. I would make it my business to know everything about her condition and together we would overcome this.

Ellie continued to fight hard, but it was more to buy time than to rid herself of this dreadful disease. One particular weekend, I had arranged for her to come down to Brighton with me to see our holiday flat. It was undergoing a complete renovation and the carpets were being put in. I knew she was frail, but I wanted her to see it in all its glory. It had been quite an achievement in renovation. It was a typical Regency property on the top floor and right by the seafront. Having had six months of renovation work, I wanted to show Ellie how things were progressing. I checked first if she was well enough. "I'll make myself well", she said, and off we went. The drive was straightforward, and I think she liked my car, although, material things were never that interesting to her. We arrived at the flat, and although weak, she was clearly impressed. Afterwards, we walked slowly along the seafront and stopped for lunch. She didn't eat anything, she just sipped a cup of hot water and talked of my future. "Now, make sure you pay off your mortgage, it's imperative that you are not beholden to anyone, especially, a bank". "I don't want you on the pill anymore, it's very bad for you". "Only eat organic food and only drink organic wine - Chilean is best". "Hold your breath when you fill up your car as petrol fumes are carcinogenic". On and on she went while I was getting more and more cross with her. "You're not going to die Ellie, so stop talking like this". But I was refusing to see what was right before my eyes. My beautiful Ellie was fading fast.

I had started a new business at around this time which was going well. It was the late 90's, and the dot com boom was just emerging. I was a co-founder in an internet start-up that was attempting to contextualise sector-specific web content. We'd just received £3m in funding and were entering into a huge growth phase which was super-exciting, if a little hectic. We began in London, but within a few months, I would move to LA where we attempted to build a bigger vision of the platform. But, at the peak of Ellie's illness, I was thankfully still working in London. I would visit her almost daily, and every time she would insist that we talk about anything else but her illness. As things progressed, she was moved into the local hospital where I locked into her daily routine. I would come every day, and each time she would protest that I should be out working, but I didn't care. I worked around her, and my colleagues understood that this was my priority. Although a short commute away, it may as well have been based on Mars, as my universe had shrunk to just this hospital room during those last precious weeks.

In true Ellie style, even her final days were filled with love and laughter. With the self-knowledge that she had little time left, she assembled all her closest friends, and we sat together in her hospital room watching home movies taken over the years. We all celebrated her prime on the screen, acutely aware that this once vital woman was about to leave us. Our hearts were all breaking, but if she could sit there smiling at the screen wide-eyed, burning her memories into her fully apertured soul, who were we to show our own agonies? No, we laughed along with her at all her antics, marvelling at her strength of character as she relived her past glories, full in the knowledge that it was all behind her with no chance of a repeat. The night before she died, I was sitting on her bed. I wasn't to know for sure that this was our last time together, but as my throat closed and my body tensed, she stared at me so intently, it felt as if she was imprinting me in readiness for the afterlife. She was weak and barely able to speak, so it was with some effort that she held my hand and said with all the strength she could muster, "Best success." I realised in that moment that she was always at the heart of my desire to achieve. I wanted her to be proud of me whether it was my music career, businesses, work or just about anything I did, her opinion of me mattered above all others.

I received the call the next day to say that she had passed peacefully. I was with her within the hour, and although the cancer had turned her once glorious alabaster skin to a shade of mustard, she looked like she was sleeping. I rearranged her bedclothes, pushed wisps of her hair behind her ears and thanked her. I thanked her for taking me into her heart when she didn't have to. She was thirty years old to my seven, and at the peak of her powers, and yet for much of the years that followed, she invested in the little girl across the road. She intuitively knew that I needed her love more than anything in the world, and in ways large and small, she did what she could to care for me and guide me to adulthood.

Post Ellie's death seemed to me to be an endless endurance test. First, there was the funeral which I wanted to sing at. I chose the song 'You've Got a Friend', and with her coffin right next to me, my throat was closed so tightly that at first, I could hardly get a sound out, but I swallowed hard and did my best, knowing that Ellie would have enjoyed it. Next came the house clearance. I was totally unprepared for the experience of handling and removing items that used to hold such life – Ellie's clothes, paintings, music, books and jewellery being some of them. It was unbearable. I was at least able to request a few things personal to me; a photo of her in the outback drinking a 'tinny', a large contemporary vase which I always loved and one of her blouses just so I had something of hers. The rest was boxed up to go to a charity shop. The house was put on the market, and it was almost too much to bear that someone else could live there.

Next, was something totally unexpected. I received a call from one of Ellie's cousins saying that a television production company working for Channel 4 had called, as they had heard that Ellie had died. Unbeknown to anyone, Ellie had taken part in a documentary about alternative therapies, and they wanted to know if I would be happy for it to air now she had passed. I thought that although it was going to be hard to watch, if Ellie had thought it important enough to take part in, then who was I to stand in the way of it being broadcast. Ellie's cousin agreed and we gave our blessing. The show aired just two weeks after Ellie died. It showed her desperate to find not just a cure, but a reason as to why this had happened to her. I suppose cancer sufferers the world over seek a reason, a way of rationalising why this sometimes, random event affected them personally. On screen, Ellie went through the whole list, and it was heart-breaking to watch her almost berate herself for her choices in life. She was hardly a hard drinking, free rolling reckless sort, so it seemed oddly misplaced.

The next part of the programme focused on her desire to try faith healing. This really surprised me as Ellie had never been into alternative therapies and had settled for more conventional chemo. However, this was shot quite late on in her illness, so perhaps she was desperate to try anything. In the film, she is seen receiving a faith healing, and given the now known outcome, it was almost too much to bear. However, nothing prepared me for the next scene.

Ellie was always strong in front of me, Always! From the moment we met until the last time I saw her, she smiled outwardly and never let her own worries enter my world. On screen, she was talking about how the cancer had now spread to her brain, and that this frightened her more than any other area that her cancer had spread to: "I can't lose my mind, I just can't." She was crying openly and clearly in a state of panic. This is not my Ellie! But it was. And in that moment, I realised her incredible sacrifice. She had put aside her own fears to protect us all from ours.

To this day, I live to impress her, I talk to her often and ask her advice. She comes to me in my dreams from time to time, and in those blissful waking moments, between sleep and wakefulness, I forget she is no longer on this earth, as she felt as present in these night-time visitations as she did growing up. I realise too, that she is who I live to live up to. Surreptitiously, I have emulated her life, and I'd like to think that if a shy little thing peeked across at me and I sensed her need for my love, I would offer it as unconditionally as Ellie did.

ANIMAL FARM

I love animals. I have had many pets during my adult years and take particular pride in the fact that each has been loved emphatically, cared for excessively and lived wholeheartedly, dying finally of old age rather than any neglect on my part. At my peak, I had 11 animals at once. Two beagles, two cats, one hamster, one giant rabbit, four chickens and a tortoise. It sounds chaotic, especially since I raised two kids amongst all of this, but it was far from it. Dogs, of course, were at the top of the tree. They had full run of the garden at all times, due to a dog flap being installed and leading into a large, enclosed area. Each day, I would walk them off the lead (anyone who's ever owned a beagle, let alone two at the same time, will know what a feat this is!), typically covering five miles a day across many acres of woodland that my house backed onto. Cats, of course, roamed the same woodland, and given that we only saw them when they were hungry, I joked to my vet that bringing them for their annual health check was a bit like funding wildlife. Next in the pecking order, (please excuse the unavoidable pun) were my chickens. They lived happily in a 10-metre x 6-metre x 2-metre-high purpose-built hen house. This was very roomy, but most days I would let them out and they would scratch around the flower beds, aiding the weeding. My giant rabbit had a 5-metre run also, but again, preferred the wide-open spaces of the back garden, and would run and leap with joy as I let her out after breakfast. Even the hamster lived in a luxury two-story purpose-built cabinet. It was the size of a large bedside table and had many compartments and exercise options. Her favourite part of the day was rolling around the house in a see-through ball, traversing the various rooms with her face pressed against the wall of this strangely effective mode of transport. My only source of shame is my tortoise, as I never managed to make a run that he didn't want to escape from, and when he finally escaped for good, I took his bid for freedom to be a personal failure.

I have been teased over the years about my level of attention and investment in the care of my animals. Some have seen it as slightly obsessive and maybe they're right. I'm certainly driven to care for as many as I can manage, and yes, I have sometimes wondered as to my motives. Do I love them so they love me back? Dogs are wonderful at this. I truly believe that it is an honour to be loved by a dog, and it's a unique relationship that is hard to explain to anyone who has not experienced the deep connection a dog provides. I suspect though, that my main driver is to ease my guilt and atone for the neglect suffered by my childhood pets.

Dad loved animals too. Well, I say "loved" because it is said that if you want to feel like Napoleon in your own home, buy a dog. Well in dad's case, he must have felt like God himself, as we never had less than three dogs and they were as attention-starved as the rest of the house. Their subsequent plays for his affection must have been quite the ego boost. Dad was full of sloppy kisses, but I never saw him walk, worm, groom or wash one. Most of them died young and badly; one was run over in front of my eyes, another died before its first birthday due to a birth defect (or being accidentally trodden on, which is what I suspected at the time, as she was stunted at birth and therefore the size of a guinea pig) one, as previously mentioned, died of a heart attack, aged four. All terrible deaths, but the one I remember most was the one that died fitting on the lounge floor, due to the anaemia inflicted by the

swarms of fleas, moving in unison like a dawn murmu-
ration, covering every inch of her little tan and white
body.

His need to receive love from another, but not
necessarily care for them, didn't stop with dogs, as my
dad was keen on keeping various other unfortunate
animals. He said he loved them, but again, the evidence
is questionable. The menagerie started with ducks, just
two manageable white poms. They were beautiful
birds. With fresh clean straw in a huge secure garden
shed, their introduction to their new home would have
been quite promising. Thankfully, they didn't last long
enough to endure the quagmire of muck and terror that
followed. At its peak, dad's flock was over 100-strong.
As the years advanced and the shed perished,
ramshackle boxes were constructed, which supplied
easy pickings for the fox. If they managed to survive the
daytime, they would very likely be taken in the nightly
raid. I have no beef with foxes, they do what they do,
which is to savage everything, everytime they get a
chance so they might return and collect their spoils
over various trips to their dens. Most people would not
be able to live with such losses, but rather than accept
defeat, dad would just go to the livestock market and
replenish. Ever keen to connect, I would go with him to
the market to help bring the new stock home. Each
entered their new home with wide-eyed promise and

were possibly grateful for a new life, only to become muddied malnourished fox food within weeks.

There were other random pets around my dad's garden. We had rabbits for a time. The rats killed most of them, and one starved to death having been forgotten about. After the foxes, rats were perhaps the most successful creatures. We had dozens of them. Big fat swaggering creatures with no fear of humans. Dad was quite relaxed about their presence, and to be honest, I don't remember feeling anything other than familiarity. Many times, I would put my hand in the grain bags and scoop one out of the way, as casually as the grain itself.

Growing up in *Dogbone St.* I loved all our dogs; Tammy, Misha, Vicky, Chloe, Ria, Sadie and my absolute favourite, Sheena. Sheena and I would walk for hours together, and when I got home, she would follow me everywhere, and most important of all, she would sleep on my bed at night. From the lot of our dogs, three of them had litters. These weren't planned events and dad didn't believe in vets, so they weren't spayed and were essentially "got at" whilst in season. I delivered all three litters myself. I became quite the expert, and although in my early teens, I knew all the signs of nesting, knew instinctively when the litter was about to arrive and what to do when each of them squeezed blindly into the world. I also did my best with the ducks. I am an early riser, so I would start the day by preparing the layers mash - a type of gruel that was mixed with cold water. Thereafter, I would replenish the grain containers, smash the ice out of the water bowls and wash out the filthy sediment that would have built up from the night before. On the weekends, I would shovel out the sheds and boxes. This was no small job; it would take much of the day and was back-breaking work, as the muck would be several inches thick and the stench was withering. I did my best to keep the muck at bay, but within a very short time, there was not an inch of our once lush garden that wasn't covered in acrid duck mess. With so many hungry mouths to feed, there wasn't a single shrub or blade of grass to offer. Before long, the garden looked more like a battle-scarred no man's land, and the house was not much better.

Every dog owner knows the awful realisation of coming through the door and discovering that their beloved pet has messed inside the house. Those occasional lapses are distressing for dogs and owners alike. I believe dogs, like pigs, like to keep themselves clean, and certainly do not choose to mess all over their own homes, but it happens occasionally. In our home, it was an everyday occurrence given that they were shut in from 8 am to 4 pm and had no choice but to use the house as a litter box. To help picture what a house would look like after just one day, I will try first to explain with numbers - we never had less than three dogs, so that's six good sized poos and 12 modest pees per day, 42 poos and 84 pees per week, 168 poos and 336 pees per month, and so on and so on. I would try and keep back the tide by putting down newspapers, but they were soon turned to mush, which just made things worse. Granny had a dog too. Danby was a neurotic overweight King Charles Spaniel. He spent the whole day chained up in Granny's bedroom, only to be seen when he needed to be dragged to the back door to relieve himself. This was a complete waste of time, as he would mark every part of the house on his way, leaving almost nothing in his bladder once the back door was opened.

The ammonia burned your eyes, and the downstairs was uninhabitable. Dad would occasionally buy a new carpet which would offer some reprieve. My eldest brother and I would try to keep it clean, but we didn't have a vacuum cleaner, so we used the toe of our trainers and scuffed away at the whole carpet until we had dehaired as much as we could. I borrowed a vacuum cleaner from a neighbour once; a very lovely family whose daughter was roughly the same age as me. I still see her from time to time. I was very grateful to not have to spend hours dragging my shoe across the mire, but my joy soon turned to shame, as, despite my best efforts to clean it post-use, I had left a streak of poo on the underside. I still reel from this story, and although dog mess was an everyday occurrence for me, to her it was outrageous. We have met several times as adults, and she never tires of re-telling this event, unaware of the renewed kick of shame I feel each time.

With dog hair, faeces, urine and general dust and dirt everywhere; in just a few short years, the house had gone from a normal suburban home to a Dickensian-Esq hovel. I managed to keep my bedroom fairly clean, but the rest of the house suffered terribly. Cold, damp, flea-ridden and noxious, it must have despaired at its turn of fortune. The previous owners may have slowed down due to their age, rendering the house in need of modernisation, but these new inhabitants leeched the very fabric of its foundations, even before granny brought it to its knees by setting fire to it.

THE GREAT FIRE

*T*he evening of the fire itself was unremarkable other than my eldest brother was home and had a new girlfriend. Showing off slightly, he offered to buy us all KFC. Off he went in his shiny Ford Cortina, and we duly waited for his return. As the only habitable rooms were upstairs, we all waited expectantly in our bedroom, and although KFC is typically a finger-licking experience, it occurred to me that we should probably have plates and cutlery, so my sister went down to the kitchen to get four sets of everything. Moments later there was a scream as she opened the kitchen door and released a huge fireball into the lounge. I was in my mid-teens and had not experienced fire before, so I turned to my brother's girlfriend, thinking she would take charge. My expectation was that she'd leap into action, but rather than take any form of crisis leadership, she just freaked out and bolted for the door, leaving my sister and me in her wake. My first instinct was to call the emergency services. Being 1985, the phone was attached to the wall - not normally inconvenient, but given that it was in the lounge that was currently on fire, it was far from ideal. Having been politely asked to "leave the burning room" by the operator, my next thought was to get the dogs out. I delegated this to my younger sister whilst I focused on getting granny.

Granny was a hoarder, her room was filled with every human detritus imaginable. She was also a boarder - of windows, and crucially, doors. Under normal circumstances, her tendency to build barricades didn't bother us - at least she was contained. During a full-blown house fire though, this was potentially deadly. I put my full weight onto her door and hoped something would give. Her typical method was to wedge an ironing board up against the door handle, so the odds were not in my favour, but at last, it opened. I think she had decided to move the ironing board herself, but it had taken effort to do so, and by the time I had reached her, the fire was raging above us. I was fully expecting compliance, given the circumstances, but when I grabbed her arm, she wouldn't budge, as her unfortunate dog was chained to the bed and out of my reach. I had no choice but to leave him to his fate and force granny out into safety. Given her advanced dementia and the fact that I wouldn't get her dog, she, of course, took this as confirmation that I was indeed a "fucking bastard woman" which was her favourite "Shiela Crickleshank" insult during her full blown demented state, and she was not shy in telling me so in that moment.

Granny was now raging at the neighbours whilst I was taking a dog roll call. Vicky, the Beagle - present. Chloe the Labrador Cross - present. Sheena my beloved Labrador - present. Phew, all accounted for, nothing to do now but wait for the fire crew to put the house out of its misery. But hold on! Did I count correctly? Chloe and Sheena look almost alike apart from their pedigree; surely, I hadn't counted the same dog twice, had I? But I had and it was Sheena that was missing. I sprinted back into the burning house with no thought other than to find her and drag her out. By this time, the fire had really taken hold, and just as I was trying to enter the front door, the fire crew arrived and pulled me back. Defeated, I had no choice but to sit on a low wall opposite the house and wait.

Whilst all this drama was unfolding, I had forgotten about the KFC. It seemed an age before my brother arrived with a Bargain Bucket in hand, just 30 minutes from when he left, such is the speed of fire. By the time he'd taken it all in, it was over. Almost two-thirds of the house was burnt, and all of it was now flooded. Having made it safe to enter, the firefighters went to look for Sheena. As if in a slow-mow movie sequence, Sheena was carried out. I was preparing for a limp, lifeless charred carcass, but to my great joy, she wagged her tail in recognition as the firefighter heroically handed her to me. He said that she must have been super-stressed as she had messed all over the bedroom they had found her in and she'd also shredded the bed. I was too ashamed to tell him that that was my dad's room, and that's how it always was. I was just elated that she had survived. Granny's dog, sadly, didn't make it. She was mad at me, but I was also mad at her. Had she not tied him to the bed, he would have had half a chance to leave the room. But, I said nothing as she repeatedly hit me over the head for the murderess act of saving her life over his.

Dad arrived much later. He was having his usual evening meal at one of his friends' houses that night, and given that this was the pre-mobile phone era, quite how the police knew how to contact him remains a mystery. Maybe I'd watched too many disaster movies, but I was expecting him to run from the police car in panicked expectation, witness the relief from seeing we were all ok, bask in his desperate bodily checks in case I was injured and be swept into his arms and declared a hero for saving everyone. I, of course, should have known better. Apparently, he just wanted to know where his mother was. I had this clarified at his funeral, where the eldest boy from this particular family, said how he always remembered that night. Apparently, the police knocked on their door and told dad his home had had a fire and that he should come with them. I waited expectantly for the rest of the story, once again having watched too many movies where the father falls to his knees and screams into the air, "my children, my children", but once again, these images were dashed. He had cried alright, but just not for us. My dad just kept repeating, "my mother, my mother", not stopping until he was assured by the police that she was safe.

If the house was in intensive care before, it was now on life-support. Barely habitable pre-fire, at least it had a kitchen and a boiler which were now destroyed. Granny's room was gutted, as was a lot of the downstairs area. Dad, my brothers, and granny had no choice but to spend the night in whatever part of the house they could make habitable. My sister and I avoided the main part of the rebuild as we were housed by a local family. This was an incredibly generous gesture, especially, given the grandness of their home. We were to share the girl's room, which again was very generous of them. We must have been quite the sight and smell when we first arrived - rather like refugees who'd travelled hundreds of miles, not 500 yards around the corner.

We settled in quite nicely, albeit strange to have a routine. Breakfast, lunches and dinners were all provided for, including clean, comfortable and warm bedding, and best of all, peace. Lots of peace! No demented rantings from my granny, no maniacal mutterings from my brother, no daily threats of beatings, and most amazing of all, a woman to look after us. It was wonderful, but sadly, short-lived. Within a few weeks, we were told we could come home. I'm not sure who was more gutted, as our temporary family had gotten quite attached to us and the mum later revealed that she didn't want to send us back, as she knew some of what was going on, but back we went.

Granny had spent the night of the fire in our old box room. Once installed, even after her room had been completely renovated, she insisted on staying where she was, thus providing my sister and I the opportunity of having her room which was much larger, and better still, completely brand new. This presented enormous creative possibilities. I had my own money as I was working part-time at the local leisure centre. An ingenious step on my part, as although it paid just £1 per hour, I had somewhere warm to be and had negotiated free lunches, access to the showers and could even wash my clothes in the laundry room. With my wages, I began creating my little haven which started with buying a carpet. Not what typical 15-year-olds choose to spend their money on, but I took it very seriously and opted for an offcut from the local carpet shop. It didn't quite fit the whole room but was enough to create a walkway between the beds. This being the mid 80's, I opted for a red and white checked duvet set and an accompanying duvet inner. In an act of sisterly generosity, I bought a set for my sister too, but this was more to complete the look of the room than pure altruism. To complete the desired effect, I placed red electrical tape across the walls in a kind of Michael Jackson Thriller-inspired zig zag. Once I was happy with the overall look, I bought a fridge for £5, a second-hand television from a friend, and best of all - a fully functioning set of spirit optics. I was very happy with mine/our new room, but the rest of the house didn't fare so well. Dad only had building insurance, so there was no money for what was lost beyond the structure itself. We could live without a functioning kitchen, given that the pre-fire one had been semi-redundant, but losing the boiler was a blow. Awful as our house was before the fire, it at least had heating.

SCHOOL OF ROCK

To the majority of children, I would imagine a typical day for a 70's kid would start with either an alarm clock or a parent shouting to say that breakfast was ready and it was time to get up. Teeth would be brushed, faces washed, uniforms would be donned, satchels checked and once everything was present and correct, an accompanied trek to school would ensue. Lessons would be had, school lunches would be eaten, and the journey home would include a general chit-chat until you entered the front door, dropped your bags, kicked off your shoes and ran to the kitchen to raid the fridge for a snack, while you waited for teatime. I, of course, am worldly-wise enough to know that this was not the case for all kids, but given that I lived in the heart of suburbia and had been on a couple of playdates, I had a sense of what "normal" looked like. My day, however, was somewhat different.

Having slept as best I could in a cold dank bedroom with no dinner in my tummy since school the day before, I would get myself dressed into my one and only school uniform, and with matted hair and unbrushed teeth, slip quietly into my sleeping dad's bedroom to grab my dinner money and walk myself to school. I didn't have breakfast at home, which must have either been noted by one of my teachers or perhaps, I was just so skinny that it was obvious, but whatever the reasoning, on reaching school, I would discreetly present myself to the back door of the kitchens where a cup of strawberry yoghurt would be handed to me. It was served in one of the school's melamine beakers, and therefore, was an enormous portion. It was so fresh tasting and thick, with fruit pieces, I don't know if it's nostalgia or reality, but I don't think I've ever found its equal since. I would then register along with all my fellow students, go to class, and promptly and regularly fall asleep on my desk, only to be gently nudged awake by my form teacher. This happened often, but I don't recall ever being punished for it. I'd like to think that they just knew that I was trying my best. Lunch was served, and with great sleight of hand, I was passed a teacher's plate followed by an extra bottle of milk. After more lessons and possibly an afternoon nap on my desk, I would trundle home, let myself in, navigate past the sea of dog excreta and take shelter in my shared bedroom. I would also walk the dogs or find someone to play out with. At some point, I would take myself off to bed, having no evening meal, just to restart the whole cycle again.

I enjoyed school but often felt that I was on the outside looking in. Not knowing how to join in with stories of brownie camps, day trips, family parties and birthday treats gave me little opportunity to bond naturally. I did bond though, and surprisingly I found myself quite popular. Intuitively, I worked out that a quick mind, a joke here and there and an overall sunny disposition - plus absolutely no mention whatsoever of what was going on at home - made me someone people wanted to know. I was also good at sports which helped my need for acceptance and belonging.

Along with sports, I was also musical. I sang the lead parts in most of the school productions and I genuinely enjoyed entertaining. I loved to sing, but sadly, my middle-school music teacher was not a big fan of mine. I'm not quite sure what went wrong, but it might have been that even though this was my favourite subject and I looked forward to each class, she taught it like it was a penance, which irritated me, and I let it show by being the class clown and was no doubt equally annoying. So, when it was time for one school production, I was relegated to percussion: no part, no songs, no dialogue, just a table of maracas, glockenspiels, tambourines, finger castanets, bells, triangles and cymbals - all standard 1970's school equipment. She probably thought I was duly punished, but her plan backfired as I had a great time. Naively she'd placed me in front. I'm sure I started respectfully enough, but before long, I was banging and crashing with gusto, and the titters from the parents started to occur in response to my antics rather than what was happening onstage. The music teacher was furious but there was nothing she could do - a star was born - well not quite, but she could hardly shoo me off the stage mid-performance, so I took this as a small victory.

After various first and middle schools, the next logical place for me to go would have been the local secondary school, which, although a little farther away, was still within walking distance. However, it was about to close, so dad enrolled me into a school that was about a half hour coach ride away. I really loved this school too - when I went to it. Being a coach ride away presented quite a big logistical challenge for me in that it left every morning at 8 am. Given that I would not get to sleep until dad came home, which could be anything up to 2 am, getting myself up, dressed and out in time for the bus was unrealistic. The school was understanding and very reasonably struck a deal - I promised I would do my best to make the lesson after morning break and they agreed, so long as I signed in so that they knew I was on the premises. Given that it started at 10.15 am, I felt quite confident I could make this commitment. I recall having spurts of real enthusiasm where I would throw myself into a subject and take part in class lessons with genuine interest, but it was usually short-lived. As my home life became more challenging, school attendance became background noise. When I did go, I enjoyed some subjects such as art, music, English and sports, but beyond the options year, it all became - well – optional.

Remarkably, I was allowed to stay on at 6th form. I imagine they reasoned that it was better for me to be kept on, even if I didn't have the requisite O Level's, than to leave and lose track of me completely. Even more surprising is that I went on to complete 2 A levels which were Theatre Studies and English. I also took Sociology, and to my shame, I didn't pass. It was not that the subject disinterested me, or that the teacher was unengaging, it was simply that it wasn't something I could just "wing". I feel bad about not trying harder, as the teacher was wonderful and helped me enormously, both inside the school and out. Again, I can only imagine that she saw someone in need and came up with her own intervention, as her particular investment in me was to pay me to do her ironing. Looking back, I was completely overpaid for this simple task, and she spent the whole time enquiring as to my wellbeing, so much so, that she might as well have done the job herself. I see now that it was her way of keeping an eye on me, as well as offering me the opportunity to earn some money.

As already confessed, there was general absenteeism, but there were some classes that I would miss specifically, Home Economics being the prime example. I remember clearly finding the whole idea of coming to school to learn, at the age of 13, what I had been doing for myself since I could remember, completely ridiculous. There was even a classroom that was decked out as a flat so we could practice the essential skills of bed-making, cleaning, and cooking. As a bonus subject, we could also do needlework. When I say we; I mean the girls. I don't recall being terribly feminist in my views, just that I thought it was tedious and boring, and what I really wanted to do was computing, metalwork and carpentry, as these were far more creative in my mind than making beds. I also avoided Home Economics class because it needed ingredients, and putting together everything needed for coq au vin was just not realistic for me. Rather than draw attention to this fact, it was best to 'bunk off'. I managed this for pretty much the whole time, but one day the teacher begged me to come to the next class. It was bread making and she felt that this would be beneficial to me. The allotted day duly came around, and of course, I didn't have any of the ingredients, but I had my dinner money, so on the way to school, I went to the local shop and bought a bread mix. Just add water - brilliant! I was quite pleased with myself for my inventiveness, but my teacher had other ideas. Suffice to say, she just thought I was disrespecting her class and I was appropriately dealt with.

Academia rarely got my attention, but there was to be a final-year concert at school. I didn't have an act as such, but I could play the bass guitar. I stumbled over this amazing instrument by chance. There was a local music shop, and on the days I was bunking off, I would spend large chunks of the day there. I was completely bewitched by all the instruments and would spend hours tinkering. The manager was very patient and must have liked me, as he sold me a Gibson SG copy bass and set up a tab that I could pay back when I could. He also gave me a powered set of headphones so I could practice at home.

However, even though I was super keen, by the time the concert came around, there was no band to show off my bass skills with, so I volunteered to sing. The music teacher at the time hadn't heard me sing before, so he insisted that I show him what I had before he committed to accompanying me. I was a skinny little thing, so it was with some surprise that I belted out a soulful rendition of Summertime by George Gershwin. I think he was genuinely shocked at the voice that came from my little frame. I had previously only sung at home, mostly to my dad's records played on his old gramophone. As I started to earn money, I built up quite a vinyl collection of my own, and was particularly keen on early reggae songs by Jimmy Cliff & UB40. I was also into chart stuff, soul music and R&B. I had one album called Working Week, which I practically wore thin through overuse. I loved every song on it, and the lead singer had a wonderfully deep soulful voice which I enjoyed singing along to. Whatever my early influences, my teacher liked what he heard and agreed to accompany me at the concert.

My first gig! What to wear? I was told that I couldn't wear my school uniform so I asked around to see what would be appropriate. Something formal was the answer I got, which was bad news, as apart from my uniform, I just had a pair of jeans and a few tops. I asked around and someone loaned me an orange corduroy over the knee length skirt. Apparently, tights would be a good idea which presented another challenge. I had never bought a pair of tights before, but I had my own money so off I went to the shops. When the big show came around, I duly went to the girls changing room. The skirt was not very flattering but would do, and at least it went with my white school blouse. I then put on my tights, but something was wrong. For some reason, they were individual legs and only came up to the middle of my thighs. I realised with panic that I had bought stockings instead of tights! The show had already started, and I was due on stage in just a few minutes. I could ditch the tights but I was embarrassed by my skinny white legs, so I set about finding another solution. I went into the nearest classroom and found some masking tape. I wound it around my legs at the top end of the stocking and then placed strips down my legs to secure them to my skin. I had only moments to spare before I was ushered backstage. This was it, my first vocal performance. I just needed to hold my nerve (and my stockings), and I would be a huge hit. My music teacher began, and I surprised everyone with my soulful sound, but as the second verse came around, I felt an unmistakable peeling sensation. The house lights were warm enough already without the added panic, sending my internal temperature soaring, and there was still the second verse to sing. My able accompanist must have thought I was just building the moment, but I was so scared of exposing my masking-taped stockings that I clean forgot how the second verse began. Like a true pro, he went round and around the second verse intro while I leant against the wall of the stage trying to look like a jazz crooner building the tension.

Tension of a different sort was starting to weaken as the masking tape peeled, but at last, the lyrics for the second verse came to me. The tempo may have taken everyone a little by surprise, but it was either double time or risk irrecoverable embarrassment. I rushed off the stage straight to the girls' loos and binned the offending items, having kept my dignity intact.

Unperturbed by my debut, I had the opportunity to join a local band as lead vocalist. We had quite a following, and when it came to my very first gig, I wasn't nervous at all, just overexcited. I've done a lot of things in my life and had many challenges and successes, but still, to this day, I would say I'm most proud of my musical achievements. Music is literally at my very core, and I particularly love live performances. In fact, I love all of it! I love how people respond to me, and I truly want them to feel entertained. When I was on stage, I didn't think about anything, and as I look back now, I realise that singing was an escape. I was out of the house, going to rehearsals and gigs, and it made me feel good; it made me feel that maybe I wasn't such a geeky, awkward, smelly, crap kid after all!

Other bands came and went until the day I met Chris. He had just completed the creation of his studio and was looking for artists, so he came to watch me sing at a local pub. I sang "Nutbush City Limits" by Tina Turner, and whether it was the incongruity of that gutsy song coming out of a skinny 16 year old or the sheer joy emanating from me on being behind a microphone, he saw something in me and asked if I would sign on with his management company.

Chris was and is an exceptional musician and knew a lot of great writers and other musicians too. I was listening to a lot of "old" music at the time, which included artists like Joni Mitchell, Rickie Lee Jones, Little Feat and Billy Cobham. These artists influenced my own writing heavily, and over some months, we produced a full album of tracks under my new stage name, "Billy Levi". My new name was chosen by Chris, as he thought, a) I looked great in jeans and b) we could do with a sponsor! I gigged in London, in venues such as the Borderline, Hard Rock Café & Mean Fiddler, and we made an album in the studio. On the album, and for the London gigs, I was accompanied by exceptional session musicians who played for bands like Go West & Matt Bianco, who were prominent artists at the time. My own band was made up of local musicians, and it was so much fun playing the pub and club circuit.

'Billy Levi' never quite became the household name we had all hoped it would, and I found myself drifting from project to project. I had some success with Nigel Wright, a producer and musical director for artists such as Madonna, Take That, Barbra Streisand and Andrew Lloyd Webber. Nigel released a single with my vocal on it, which was a cover of the Four non Blondes classic, "What's Up". It was a fun experience and reached the heady heights of number 72 in the charts, but there was no follow-up. I did a few more projects which included recording a dance remix of Right Said Fred's "Swan", but their label decided not to release it, and slowly and surreptitiously, my singing career faded into the background, as my work career took off. That said, I made quite a lot of money as a songwriter. My most notable and profitable success was writing a B Side and album track for The Osmond Boys, not quite as famous as their parents, but it sold well.

I still sing now and then, mostly for friends or at events, and I still love it. As the years passed, I turned my musicality to helping others, firstly as CEO of a major music institute in the UK, then opening a series of youth music academies, followed by being headhunted to set up a music institute in India. And as for Chris, he is still my soul mate and number one fan. I may not have made it to the big time, but I found my best friend, and that's more than good enough for me. Chris has loved and supported me through over thirty years of trials and tribulations and knows me better than anyone. We are as close today as we have ever been, and I love him wholeheartedly and can't imagine life without him.

THE WOMEN IN MY LIFE

I have spent most of my life fascinated and in equal measure, fearful of women. They represent a great yearning in me, which I used to find uncomfortable. I felt attracted and repelled in the same instant, rather like powerful magnets. At first, it was mother figures, with Ellie being the most significant, but there were also school friends' mums, dinner ladies, teachers; and pretty much all the women around me held some level of emotional pull. I would watch how they'd bend to reach down to their own children and scoop them up in their arms, place their hair behind their ears, touch their backs, brush their cheeks, or bury their faces into their necks and breathe them in. I wondered while hearing from friends, how they had magical stories read to them, or better still, made-up ones told with gusto to ignite the imaginations of their sleepy audience. I treasured sleepovers, never wanting them to end, and marvelled at the attention granted to me and my friends by their parents, and in particular, their mothers. With dinner served, baths run, pyjamas laid out, teeth brushed and night nights said, we crawled into crisp clean beds, and I would watch with an ache in my heart, the good night kisses and soft eyes laid on my friend from her mother. My heart would almost burst with longing, and yet, I settled with just being close to these miraculous matriarchal figures, breathing them in before the light went out. Dinner ladies were perhaps my first maternal crush. I would seek them out from the moment I could descend on the school playground. I think they knew that all I needed was to be close to them. I never asked for anything other than proximity, and they were happy to let me trail around them like a lovelorn puppy. I was equally doe-eyed around the kitchen staff. I always boasted that I never missed a day of school from my early school years, but it would be more accurate to say that I never missed a school meal, as this would have been the real motive behind my presenteeism. It was the only food I would have that day, with the added bonus of all these soft-skinned, floral-smelling, beautiful women, I was not going to miss it for anything.

My early school years' relationships were straightforward enough. School uniforms are perfect for hiding social division, and my secret shame at my home situation was largely limited to a few eagle-eyed staff members; the bullies on the playground thankfully, had not discovered my numerous weaknesses. In fact, I worked hard to hide them. I would play the class clown, the clever, quick-witted one to make them see past my dirty shoes, greying socks, outgrown uniform, and unwashed state. I was never bullied at school, in fact, it was quite the opposite, as I was seen, celebrated and loved even. It was where I felt safe, secure, warm and fed, much like home life for most of my peers. Secondary school female friendships were a little more complex. I had my first teacher crush in English class. Smart, funny, warm and with a calm authority, I would look forward to each lesson, partly to learn, but mostly to be around her. I recall editing one piece of work, almost line by line, with each correction requiring an in-person discussion as to the merits of almost every word. Maybe she knew that I needed to be near her, to experience the warm glow she emitted. I'll never know, but I will always be grateful for her investment in me.

I was spending more and more time at the leisure centre where I became very good friends with two older girls. They were both in the year above me and at a different school, so it was an unlikely alliance. One was a great badminton player and spent a lot of her time training at the leisure centre. The other was and still is a striking, six-foot blonde, Dutch woman. I don't see her so much these days, but my badminton-playing pal, although having retired her racquets years ago, is still very much in my life. Both these girls gave me a much-needed boost of self-esteem. They welcomed me into their 'older' world and gave me instant kudos.

My best friend at secondary school was what would have been known then as a "swot", but looking back, I can see that she was just incredibly bright. We both attended Bishop Reindorp, which sounds rather posh, but it was otherwise known as Guildford C of E, and has now been almost entirely rebuilt and renamed Christ's College. It used to look like a classic 1960s block, with a three-storey building typical of its type. It now looks more like a Borstal, so I'm not sure if that's progress. It boasted nothing, other than it had its own ski slope, which is still operating today. It was also known for enthusiastic skirmishes with nearby Park Barn School, which was no mean feat, given their fearsome reputation.

All the forms were named after cities, with cathedrals such as Durham, Canterbury and York, etc. I was in Durham, which had the most delightful Form Tutor. I hope he's still alive somewhere, enjoying a wonderful retirement, as he was a very special teacher. With infinite patience and a gift for nurturing, he was an absolute treasure, and very popular in the school. My very academic bestie and I were not an obvious partnership, as I was prone to showing off and rule-breaking, while she was shy and studious. She had a very gentle spirit, and I can picture her blonde hair and beaming smile to this day. Her generosity was limitless, and as well as helping me keep up on missed lessons, she also shared her lunch, which always had the same ingredients - cracker wheat with cheese spread, fruit and a biscuit, and although it wasn't much, I always got half of it. I don't know if we discussed my being hungry all the time, or if she just noticed and then offered out of natural humanity, either way, I was very grateful. Sharing her food was incredibly generous and something I have never forgotten, but perhaps, her greatest gift to me, was sharing her mum.

Her mum was my deepest "friend's mum crush" because she epitomised everything I thought having a mum would be. She adored her children as well as her husband, "Hoth" (head of the house as he used to joke), and they adored her back. They were such a happy family that I fell in love with the whole package. Over time, I got to know the aunties and cousins too, and the joy of joys, I was invited to go on a camping holiday with them, which was my first ever holiday, and I loved it. Come to think of it, this must be why I love camping so much today. I have camped out several times each and every year since the children were toddlers, and I just love it. Each year, we always stay at the same campsite, same pitch and with the same group of friends. The owners, Bill and Helen, are the nearest thing I have to an uncle and aunt, and the friends we see there are as important to me as family. I am sure this annual pilgrimage is more than just a holiday, and perhaps the root of this passion is due to these early holiday experiences.

We kept in touch for many years after we left school. I called her up some years ago to find out that she had a daughter whom she named Julia. I was so taken aback that I didn't dare ask if it had anything to do with our friendship. Deep down, I hoped it did. The next time we spoke was when she called me to say that her mum was dying of cancer. I literally said what little I could muster and put down the phone and cried. I didn't call her for some time after that, afraid of what she might have said to me. I heard once that people are alive until you are told otherwise and I wanted to keep her alive for as long as I could, so I avoided the inevitable by just not calling. I felt terribly guilty for being so selfish, but I just couldn't comfort my friend because I was so scared, myself. I also felt that I had no right to such feelings, and that it would just make things worse if I called up. Either way, it was some time before I knew for sure that she had died. She was the first of my friends' mums who had gone.

I eventually left school with not much more than fond memories, and although I will always think of all of my school friends warmly, over time, we grew slowly apart, as I found my way in the world of work.

I've always been a grafter. From cleaning out the duck pens for my dad, to holding back the mire at home as best as I could, I have always been hard working, and tried to do my very best. In my early entrepreneurial days, work was more a procurement and safety exercise – food, clothes-washing, dry and safe places to be and a sense of belonging somewhere, were necessary by-products of any endeavour.

My formal work life started with what I would call "the hustle". In the early days, I didn't have a plan as such, I was more just the opportunist, but when I saw something that I could potentially do, I was not shy in asking if help was needed. With school very much optional by the age of fourteen, I had managed to secure myself multiple paid jobs, particularly, at the leisure centre which was becoming a bigger part of my life. My main role was as a sports assistant which largely involved putting out badminton nets and doing light cleaning. I also still worked in the restaurant and came up with an entrepreneurial idea to help the management with a rather delicate problem, while I tried to revise for the few exams I was taking.

It's all changed now, but there was a time when the sauna area of the leisure centre was situated in the farthest corner of the complex. This was in an era before CCTV, and the comings and goings in this area were impossible to monitor. This suited the gay community very well, and word soon got around that it was a haven for cruising. We found this out during maintenance work when the panels in the ceiling were removed, only to reveal a stash of sex toys. The solution? I suggested to the management that if they were happy to pay me £1 per hour, I would sit outside the doors of the sauna and hand out towels and locker keys. It was hardly high-tech surveillance but the presence of a member of staff just feet away from the door seemed to do the trick, and the sauna became a plain old sauna once more. I on the other hand got paid to do my revision and washing, and there was a free lunch thrown in. Perfect!

I learnt much in these early roles. Selling fruit and veg in the local market taught me how to banter like a pro. It also taught me mental arithmetic, as did bar work, given it was well before the digital age and complex orders had to be worked out in my head and in an instant. Both bar work and market stalls also instilled resilience. Standing on my feet all day in all

kinds of weather certainly tested my resolve, particularly, in the extremes of summer and winter. The
former was typified by bee stings from the fruit and
heat strokes from the sun, while the latter would render
my body so cold that I would wrap myself in a duvet
when I got home before I took a bath, so I could get
some feeling back, and therefore reduce the risk of
scalding myself.

There were other early roles that played their parts.
There was the local jean store where I mostly just
folded t-shirts all day, the pharmaceutical company that
needed Petri dishes washed-up by hand, the various
kitchen washing-up roles as well as numerous office
temp jobs that barely lasted a week or two, but I didn't
mind as at least I was earning.

My first proper office role was at a local computer
peripheral distribution company named CPU. The role
was for an office coordinator, and I had no idea what a
computer peripheral distributor did, but I was going to
give it my best shot. I called my music manager, Chris,
who knew more about these things and he did his best
to coach me on the technical and commercial merits of
hard disks, floppy drives, tape backup and various
other items that were 'alien' to me. I also went to their
trade reception and pretended I was a local computer
dealer and asked if I could please have a brochure. I
studied hard and felt fully prepared. Only one thing to

do next, and that was to think of something to wear. I can still picture my interview outfit. What a sight I must have been. A brown shin-length skirt with a green and brown cropped top and a white t-shirt underneath, and a pair of leather, latticed court shoes. I must have looked quite a sight in front of my interviewers. However, whether it was pity or the fact that I knew more about their products than expected, they offered me the job. I loved working there. It was my first taste of office life with all its community and camaraderie. I laughed a lot during my five years there. I saw a lot of changes, made loads of friends and drank large amounts of beer. Social drinking hadn't really been a feature before, but with the advent of a steady wage and an after-work drinks culture at the local bar, I soon became quite an accomplished boozer. I worked hard too, as the saying goes, but to me, it wasn't hard graft, and certainly nowhere near as challenging as holding down three jobs simultaneously.

There were many strong characters; with the sales Director, Jan, by far the most influential. She was barely thirty years old when I met her, but she was business battle-scarred already and had an iron will. She taught me not only to work hard and believe in my abilities but also how to party and swear with gusto. She was every inch the archetypal eighties-styled business-woman. She wore Armani suits and was very direct, with a few trademark sayings such as her message to new recruits which was FIFO (fit in or f**k off). Once at a particularly high stress meeting, she told the entire management team, "I've revised the end of month targets down, and to be honest, if you can't hit these new numbers you're a bunch of c**ts." Suffice to say, we all gave it our best. She lived life like it was ending any minute, and given the fact that she had sky-dived over eight hundred times, she was probably wise to do so. The only person more supercharged was the managing director. Together, they were such a power-house couple, and have since married and gone on to forge the most incredible life together. They're still very much in my life and I consider them family. They have three amazing girls, several Great Danes and the most beautiful property. More than that, I have never before, or since, met two people so perfectly suited. CPU has long since closed its doors but I keep in touch with a few of my good friends there, the most significant of all being Kate.

Kate and I met when I had just turned eighteen, and she, seventeen. I had moved into a local bedsit close to CPU and we became firm friends. She was, and still is, stunning. With natural blonde hair, great big blue eyes, and brilliant white teeth, she looks like a cross between Cameron Diaz and Elisabeth Moss. She seemed to always radiate good health, which was curious, given that her appetite for drinking excessively rivalled even the local rugby club, a member of which she ultimately married. I was totally bedazzled by Kate. She was extremely confident and seemed completely unselfconscious in everything she did. At the age of seventeen, she already had her own flat in a very well to do area, and we had many great parties there. Where I was just getting to grips with how to match tops with trousers, she was wearing designer labels with her own twist. Sassy and confident, in truth, I was and still am, very much in awe of her. Both our careers took various pathways, and later, after more than thirty years, we reconvened and are currently working together once more, this time not in IT, but in the heady world of Private Equity.

Later on in life, I had befriended several other key women. There was Bekki whom I met when I was Managing Director of a multimedia firm. At just twenty six, I was tasked with looking after the UK operation which was no small task in that, I reported directly to the President of the European arm of the company that globally had annual revenues in excess of $1.4bn. I was responsible for a mere $50m of this sum, but at twenty six, this was a huge responsibility and Bekki was a great support to me during some of the harder moments of my four years in their employ. The most trying episode was when I blew two discs in my lower back due to all the international travel. She made sure I took great care of myself during this time, as well as many other acts of kindness that made it all the more heart-breaking when she emigrated to Australia. She lives in Brisbane now and we've grown apart, but for a long while, we were very close.

Then there's Jo, a leadership coach with a lively personality. We bonded over shoes. I was due to meet The Duke of Kent at a Prince's Trust Awards Dinner. I was part of a regional board that helped young entre- preneurs start their businesses. The dinner was very formal and I didn't know what to wear, shoe-wise. I was looking for something beige to go with my cream suit and was in the local Russell and Bromley when I spotted this very glamorous woman in tight burgundy jeans trying on red high-heeled leather boots. I had never worn anything so striking in my life and was in awe of her confidence. On a closer look, I recognised her from the school run, as she had a daughter the same age as my son. I said hello, and sought her advice on what I should buy. She screwed up her face at the mention of anything neutral and pushed a pair of striking leopard print loafers into my hand. I wasn't convinced, but judging by the compliments I received that night; she was right, and our friendship for life was secured. Now onto Yvon. Yvon literally makes me spit out my food with laughter as she has a devilish sense of humour and looks for mischief in almost every situation. She's been there for me in all my darker moments, and I call her "sis", as not only do we look alike, but she knows things about me that only a sister would share.

One of my most enduring relationships is with a couple who were friends with my mum long before motherhood took her down. They lived in a wonderful house in the middle of the woodlands. The house was like something from a wartime documentary, all cosy and unchanged with a log burning fire that heated the whole place and a wonderful back garden full of home-grown vegetables and fruit. They had three children; the eldest was very mischievous and funny and the middle girl was the image of her mum, delicate with refined features. She was a little more aloof than her gregarious older sister but I was very fond of her all the same. Then there was the youngest who was my favourite. He was the same age as me and we would play for hours in the woods collecting shotgun shells or golf balls that were miss-hit from the local course.

My most significant memories were her attempts at keeping my mother's memory alive. She was the only person in my life who wanted to talk about her. In truth, there wasn't a lot to say, but I enjoyed what little she wished to share. Her most generous gift though, was inviting us to tea on Boxing Day. I still find it astounding that this family, who were not even related to us, would invite us year after year into their home and share such a very special day on the calendar. Her husband died recently, but just before he passed, I went to see him. He was upstairs in their bedroom and I sat on the end of his bed as we talked. He was dying and he knew it. What followed was one of the most profound conversations of my life. He was crying as he started to apologise for not doing more for us. He berated himself for not calling the authorities or making dad more accountable. "I begged him to go home to you all," he said. "We would finish our badminton match and I would tell him to go home to you, but he wouldn't, he always went on to his friends. I often thought I would call the authorities but was scared that they would take you away and that I would never see you again, nor you each other, and I couldn't do it. I feel that I let you down though, as, if I had been braver, your young lives would have been so different." I let him finish as each word was said with such effort and he needed to get it all out, and then, I reassured him that he did exactly the right thing in keeping us together. I reminded him of all the Boxing days that we shared and how wonderful he was, and that I wished he could have shared his angst with me earlier in his life so I could reassure him way before his was about to come to an end.

A FEW GOOD MEN

Writing about the women in my life is easy, as they were and continue to be wonderful. I cherish each one of them, and although complex for me, they have enriched my life in a myriad of ways. There are many good men out there too, and I have been fortunate to meet several whom I have taken into my heart, but sad as it is to write this, I have also experienced the very worst of the male species.

The good ones have been extraordinary. My first man-crush was at roughly the same time as my first woman-crush with Ellie. I was eight years old at the time and Brian was in his mid-forties. However, I didn't care about the age difference and told him often that I would marry him one day. He still has a picture signed by me that says, "To the handsomest man in Essex", as it was an attempt to confirm my devotion. In this particular photo, I have a goofy grin, terrible haircut and a thin yellow roll neck stretched over a shirt, the outline of which you could clearly see through the jumper. Brian, back then, had floppy hair and a lopsided grin, and when he blew raspberries into my tummy, I squealed with delight. He was Ellie's cousin and came to visit from time to time. He may not have held quite so much intrigue for me as she, but I loved him all the same. He would invite my sister and I to his place in Essex, a gorgeous ranch-style home, complete with wagon-wheel on the front drive where he would cook for us and we would sleep in comfortable beds. Best of all, he would let us play with his drum set! He also let me drive his ford Granada, when in truth, he confessed much later that he would keep his little finger on the wheel to ensure my safety. I always felt safe with him and love him still. He may be 90 now, but he's still very much in my life and very much the handsomest man in Essex. I asked him recently how he squared it with my dad to take his two daughters away for the weekend. "Oh, I never met your dad." he'd said. I guess even if he'd wanted to ask my father, he would have had to track him down somehow as he was rarely home. So, he just assumed that it had been squared by my eight-year-old self, and I, for one, was not going to ruin any possibility of time with him.

It wasn't until I was sixteen that I found another good one. He ended up being my husband and deserves a chapter all to himself, but he would hate that. So, I will summarise everything by saying, for over thirty three years he was my protector, partner, and co-parent, and most of all, there's something I value more than anything, which is the fact that he was my greatest source of stability, particularly during those early years when all I needed was security and kindness which he provided. Despite his own demons, he dedicated his life to his children and me. I may scrub up well at this age, but at sixteen, I was far from anyone's ideal when it came to girlfriend material, and yet, he would cycle five miles each way with a plated-up dinner perched on his pannier bag and walk over a sea of dog mess to make sure I ate each night. He struggled with much of where I came from over the years, but always kept a kind of stoic neutrality where my dad was concerned; never being rude but also never building a relationship as he held him in so low regard that he didn't want to be a hypocrite. His greatest act of service was to enter the house at all, particularly my dad's room, where once or twice he was asked to fix some IT problems. Without even a face mask or gloves, he ventured into, what to anyone let alone someone from a normal middle-class home, would be a disgusting experience. My dad's room was by far the most extreme version of the rest of the house as he would have the dogs sleep with him all night and wee where they liked, which included the bed itself. The floor was bare boards that were spongy under foot, due to the constant wetness and dog mess everywhere. Worse than all of that was the thick, acrid layer of dog hair and dirt that lay over almost every surface. All of this would have been an assault on all his senses and yet, he would enter, fix what needed to be repaired, and say no more about it, so as not to embarrass me. We didn't make it to a complete happily ever after as we separated recently but, he is still very much in my life and I will be forever grateful to him for seeing beyond the mire and into the heart of someone who so dearly needed to be loved and looked after.

Knowing my ex-husband led me to meet his best friend from his early school days. He is one of the most interesting people you could hope to know. He is a black belt 3rd dan, graphic artist, watchmaker, professional photographer and guitarist, making him the epitome of a modern-day renaissance man. He's the godfather and named guardian in my will to my children, such is the trust and respect I have for him. Over the years, he has been a steadfast and dependable friend and his photographs are literally a pictorial index of my life.

My next good man was a dear colleague. I say "was" as he is no more. He took his own life when he was in his early fifties and I miss him terribly. He looked very much like Karl Pilkington and was equally warm and funny. We worked together for over ten years, and his death was a devastating shock to everyone, most of all to his wife and three kids. Through a surreal set of circumstances, we were no longer business partners and had not been in touch for a few months, but his death hit me as if we had just left the office the day before. When you work closely with someone as we had, bonds are created, making it a special relationship. I truly believe that a colleague's love is no less meaningful than that of a friend. You share so much time together, laugh together and often struggle together that it becomes inevitable for close bonds to form. We will never know what happened but I hope that he has finally found peace. I also wish with all my heart that he had made a different decision that day.

Lastly, I would like to celebrate my dear friend Chandy. We first met in London as he was setting up a Western music institute in Mumbai and had heard great things about the one I was running in the UK. Having heard many stories from dad about this wondrous city, I didn't hesitate to fly over and see what help I could offer. I spent a week with Chandy and the investors and I can still remember clear as day, the both of us sitting in a bar on the eve of my return back to the UK with a big decision to make. "So, tell me, are you going to join us?" he said, with typical Chandy directness.

"I don't know, it's all so much to take in, where will I live, how will I get around, how will we make this work with my family?" I was excited but panicking as it was such a leap of faith.

Chandy replied, "Jules, these are small problems that we can sort, the key question is, do you want to do this?" Of course I did, and I am so glad I made this decision as it led to the most extraordinary four years of my life. Chandy was at all times there to support me and I loved him dearly, then and now.

I almost shied away from this next part of the chapter, preferring to focus only on the good men in my life and dismiss my bad experiences as nothing of note. I contemplated excluding those who harmed me by what they did, as I'm sure they must have had their demons to negotiate with, or perhaps I just wanted it to not be so, that somehow if I didn't write it down, it can't have happened. But most truthful of all, I carried their shame as my own and just wanted to bury it all in the past. It's a curious thing, shame, an emotion of secrets, a deep darkness that lurks within you, burning into your soul with a temperature of its own. Shame, along with lust, envy, jealousy, and greed sit deep within us, kept down at all costs. Therefore, it's no surprise to me that most of us will not discuss the things we are most ashamed of, even if we were the victim of someone else's act. It's why it has taken me to my late middle age to discuss my own experiences.

Today, it would be called grooming, but to me back then, it was enjoying a Saturday afternoon watching the races and betting on the horses. Grandad was a great tennis player in his day. Lean, handsome and athletic, he won many a tournament in his beloved India, and this provided several trophies for me to collect for betting on the right "pony". He was also an accomplished saxophone player, and during the war, fought bravely in Burma to push back Japanese forces. He was all of these things, but to me, he was just my grandad and I loved hanging out with him when I could. I would perch myself on his sofa, dangling my little legs over the side, and shout encouragement at the horses on the telly. I have a few photos of me at this age, in fact, I only have two of them. In one, I'm at a party, and where all the girls had pretty dresses, I had what looks like a floral trouser suit. I still don't like wearing dresses because they represent a type of vulnerability to me. This is because there is too much exposure which makes for easy access. Maybe that's what they were originally designed for. A quick "lift and poke", as one of my male friends once joked, but I didn't laugh. I can't say for sure if anything happened in my earlier years, but as already detailed, my childhood was like a Rolodex, founded on each house move, and I therefore know that I was at least seven when my grandfather felt sufficient confidence in offering my 5-year-old sister and me a deal. To us, it seemed reasonable, welcomed even, as we had no other means of obtaining things for ourselves. So, it looked quite ridiculous that for just holding this shrivelled little thing that appeared harmless enough, dangling from his trouser front for just a few minutes, we would be treated to a trip to the local sweet shop to choose whatever we wanted. Had we not been so young, I'm sure we would have realised that this was basically prostitution, but as it was, we saw it as nothing more than an opportunity.

Maybe this is the source of my shame as I was complicit in the deal. I agreed to the terms and undertook the activity of my own free will, and going to the sweet shop with all its jars laid out behind the previously out of reach counter was thrilling. Grandad was very generous; whatever we wanted, we got. I think I even looked forward to his visits as I knew the day would end with Sherbet Dabs, Pink Shrimps, Lemon Bon Bon's or Cola Cubes. Not bad for such a brief encounter and what was the harm in it? I remember joking when I was in my early twenties about "handling my Grandad's todger for sweets", as if it was something that should naturally happen every day. I was at lunch with some colleagues and the conversation turned to something vaguely relevant and I just blurted it out in what I remember to be quite a comedic moment. The table fell silent and one of the party said something like, "um, that's not ok. Did that really happen?" Suddenly, aware that everyone was looking at me with forks half raised to their open mouths, I replied that of course it didn't! I was just messing around and apologised for my poor taste in humour. It's taken almost 25 years after that incident for me to mention it again, and once more, I thought perhaps I'd just leave it as it wasn't that big a deal. But it was of course. It was, because, here was an adult, completely aware of the numerous challenges his two granddaughters were already struggling with, assuming with entitled ease that we were for his gratification, available to him to satisfy his urges, and yes, he may have rationalised it as a mutually beneficial arrangement given the payment method, but it was wrong, wrong, wrong and I will not protect his shame and carry it as my own. I suspect this is in the back of all abusers minds, and especially groomers. They confuse the minds of their prey to such an extent that they take on their own sense of responsibility for what happened. Once the shame is revealed, we bury it deeply so that no one will ever know our part in it. Lung cancer eventually broke our contract. He died just one month after my mum. He was 70 at the time and had chain smoked for his whole adult life. Karma? Maybe.

There was a brief reprieve between the ages of 10 and 12. With the only family member (gosh, I just realised the dual meaning of this word in this context!) causing me any such bother now gone, I was left in peace. Perhaps it was out of respect for my recent bereavement or the fact that my trousers were trussed with tighter and thicker belts. Whatever the reason, I had a couple of years of relative peace, but it was short lived. At around 13 years old, I started "dating" a boy from a few streets away. He was nothing to look at and I don't think I even liked him that much, but, he had a nice dog at least. He had just started having involuntary erections too (my boyfriend that is, not the dog!), and this was very unsettling for me, as my grandad, for all its wrongness, merely presented a flaccid little worm that I had to deal with. This was a whole new world of size and persistence. Nothing happened beyond him just wanting to show it to me, which he did often, and I would dutifully smile at it like I was admiring his pet, which I suppose I was. Once he was satisfied that I had shown him due admiration, I went to visit his actual pet, which was far more attractive in my eyes.

This went on for some weeks and I think I just liked having somewhere else to go as it felt a little like being part of a family. So, when his elder brother who was in his mid-twenties and had two kids of his own asked me to babysit for him, I was happy to do so, as I also got paid £3 for an evening of essentially watching television whilst his kids slept upstairs. There was also the bonus of him being a local darts player, and he would invite me and his younger brother along to local tournaments. This went on for several weeks and I was so used to the routine of watching him, that I barely noticed he'd stopped asking his younger brother to come with us, so it just became something we did together. I also don't think I noticed the presence of his hand on my knee as we drove to the pub. I certainly didn't move it off my thigh as he was the local semi-pro darts player, a big shot to my nonentity self, and perhaps, this is just what big brothers of boyfriends did – a kind of fraternal protection for his younger siblings' beau. It may have started with a friendly pat on the knee, but before long, each drive to the pub would be accompanied with his hand inside my teenage knickers. I let it go as he seemed to enjoy himself and always bought me a bottle of coke and crisps when we got to the tournament. He and I settled into this routine; neither of us speaking about its meaning, but more that it was just accepted as part of the experience. I'm very confident of the age I was at this time, as 'Come on Eileen' played constantly on the radio and was a big dance floor hit. At 13 years of age, the irony of the lyrics was not lost on me then, nor now. How cute or how horrific the lyrical content depended on your personal experience with sex. To some, it was the epitome of teenage first love, while to others, it signified male predatory lust. I've never liked this song.

The routine came to a very abrupt ending one evening. I had just turned 13 and was babysitting his kids whilst he and his wife went to the pub. I had just put them to bed and turned around to find him standing at the top of the stairs, naked and fully erect. He told me to go into his bedroom as he was going to "fuck me". With him blocking the stairs, it came to me that I should move towards him and play along. Whether it was guardian angels or my instinctual survival skills honed over many years, whatever the source of my inspiration, I just pushed him back against the wall at the top of the stairs, and in a moment of self-preservation, grabbed his naked penis. He assumed, I'm sure, that I was about to indulge him. I guess the idea of a 13-year-old having this much sexual experience entered into his distorted mind, so he didn't push me back. This gave me a millisecond to manoeuvre him slightly to the left, leaving the stairs exposed behind me, thus providing an escape route. I flew down them and bolted out of the front door before he'd even had a chance to react. I've often wondered what would have happened had I not had this presence of mind. He was a large-built man, and given our lengthy "courtship", he may have assumed he was perfectly entitled to entertain himself with my body. I'm sure he was incredulous that I had tricked him at the top of the stairs. My younger self may have even felt guilty at denying his urges, but of course, my older self judges him as a predatory paedophile with a nose for the vulnerable whom he groomed over time, judging perfectly that her need for attention and naiveté would be the perfect breeding ground for his depravity. He was right of course, but as I said, I don't know what drove my actions, but that night at least, he wouldn't get his way.

I often wonder why I didn't go to the police, after all, if he did it to me, surely he wouldn't stop there, and I had a duty to protect other young girls. But, I didn't tell a soul. Like many young girls, we were conditioned by the times. Calvin Harris's hit, "It was acceptable in the 80's" means outrageous fashion to some, but to many girls of this time, it carries an undertone of the acceptability of older men having sex with young girls. Pop stars of the day openly flaunted the idea of, "the younger the better", and catcalling on the street from builders was expected by all school girls. Delightful phrases like, "old enough to bleed, old enough to butcher" were commonplace, and girls talked proudly of "losing it" at the first opportunity, almost as a rite of passage, but sometimes it was just to get it done. With all of this backdrop, is it any wonder that a fully grown man sought to have his needs met by a 13-year-old girl? I'm not excusing him, what he did was wrong, but I guess I'm excusing myself. I didn't tell anyone, as I was ashamed and felt that no-one would be at all interested. I'm sure he made the same calculation when assessing my likely response to that night's events. I don't know for sure as I never saw him or his younger brother again.

Other skirmishes followed. There was the local middle-aged accountant. Well into his forties but still a keen athlete, he took my 14-year-old self under his wing to teach me badminton at the local leisure centre. He was a good coach and he didn't take any payment as he thought I had potential. I assumed he meant my playing, but as he leaned across to kiss me full on the mouth when he dropped me off at home, I realised he meant a rather different potential. I gave up badminton rather than endure his bearded slobbering self. He's dead now, but I always hated how he presented himself as a respectable member of the community rather than the sexual predator he truly was. Again, though, I said nothing.

I met my first proper boyfriend at 15. He was 17 at the time and had a car and a job and was a talented basketball player. He wasn't classically handsome but had a good physique and an easy charm. We hung out mostly at the leisure centre which at the time was very much my second home. He made me laugh and treated me well, so I began to relax around him, and on the rare occasion his parents weren't home, we would fool around in his bedroom. First base, then second, but I wouldn't let it go any further, much to his frustration. He worked part-time at the local supermarket whilst I worked part-time at the leisure centre. Before the days of mobile phones, I got a call from the front office saying that I should call him. Fearing that he'd met with some sort of accident as he'd never asked me to call him at work before, I called immediately and asked him what was wrong. I shouldn't have worried, well, not about his wellbeing at least, as he was calling to say that there was a girl at the shop who'd said she'd be happy to have sex with him, so he wanted to ask if I would like to counteroffer and have sex with him that evening before he accepted her offer. Again, I don't know what protected me from agreeing to this obscene transactional request, but something inside me said that I had to protect myself, so I replied with, "Do what you need to do." He did and we broke up. It was a short and not very sweet first experience.

These are the villains but I truly believe they are the minority. History has done much to pit the sexes between each other, but I'm hopeful that the sea change we are seeing will continue to drive us closer together as we start to realise that Men are not from Mars and Women not from Venus, but that we're both of this Earth, and what connects us is far deeper and more enduring than history has revealed thus far.

MOTHERHOOD

Motherhood took me by surprise. I don't mean that I didn't know how babies were made, more that I never thought I would have children. I resigned myself in my twenties to be the world's favourite auntie as I'd never had the biological pull that my female friends endlessly talked about, especially as they headed into their 30's. I was so career minded and not at all interested in domesticity. I used to joke that our kitchen existed purely to house the coffee machine, and that I had never ever done a weekly shop. No, motherhood was most definitely for other people, and yet, after a typical lunch with one of my high-flying female friends, I found myself disturbed by her bliss. We had known each other a long time; she being a successful owner of a PR firm and me a partner in a business development company. We were having one of our regular al fresco lunches in trendy Notting Hill, and as I cooed and cuddled her new-born daughter, I found myself wistfully saying, "I don't seem to have any interest in practically anything right now. I have a brand new Mercedes, I'm dressed in a designer suit, I have the latest mobile phone right here and yet I feel empty inside."

She looked at me thoughtfully and said, "You need to have a baby." These few words hit me for six. This idea consumed me. It was all I could think about, and out of nowhere came this deep understanding of what my body was for, what all those periods meant and what I was destined to be. I was not on the pill at the time as I had made a promise to Ellie that I would come off it as it featured quite heavily on her "Thou shalt not get Cancer!" Ten Commandments. So, when the idea shifted from theoretical to practical, it was simply a case of throwing away the Persona hormone tracking device and just see what happens. Like many first-time mums, I was expecting conception to take its time. I had envisaged month after month of hopes dashed before the final red line shyly appeared, so, it was a massive wonderful shock when, within the first month of "trying", there it was.

I took to pregnancy much as I had taken to almost everything in my life to date. I was completely absorbed in learning everything I could about what was happening within my body. I read just about every pregnancy book available and spent many hours holding my belly and wondering what he or she was up to. I was a little apprehensive about what was to come as I had recently seen a back specialist. I had herniated two discs in my lower back during my early twenties, and at around the same time that I was obsessing about motherhood, I was also seeing a back surgeon who said, "Whatever you do, don't get pregnant right now as I'm not confident you will be able to carry." Whoops! Back issues aside, I took pregnancy in my stride. My skin had never looked so good, my hair was lush and I felt so powerful as my ever growing belly writhed under my elasticated waistband. As the date approached, I became restless, as I couldn't wait to meet my baby.

One of my best girlfriends at the time had just given birth naturally at home. She was aided by a private midwife and raved about the intimacy of the whole pregnancy and birth. Having no mother to draw upon, I thought it would be amazing to have my very own midwife to support me. I also really don't like hospitals. I know I'm not alone in this, but when friends were discussing where they would feel most safe and said that in hospital with all the gadgets was where they felt most reassured, I felt quite the opposite. I wanted to be home, surrounded by familiarity and friends. I was just

20 mins from the hospital and felt I was not taking any undue risks as it would take this amount of time if not more to prep any room, even if I were in the maternity ward itself. So, I booked my midwife who guided me expertly through each stage of pregnancy and the ultimate birth of my beautiful daughter.

I said that motherhood took me by surprise, post birth, the biggest surprise to just about everyone was how much I loved being a mum! Yes, there was fatigue, exasperation, many, many bodily aches and pains, much doubt and heartache, but there was equal joy, wonder, connection and love. I had never felt this much love in my life. I couldn't stop looking at her. She was born in my bed, and on her very first night in December, she lay next to my naked body, fitted in nothing but tiny gloves to stop her scratching her face, warmed by my body heat as she snuggled under my arm. I was completely captivated by her. This glow lasted for days as I fed her, bathed her and held her in complete love and awe. It was then that it hit me. So, this was what everyone talked about. This was the thing that everyone consoled me about when my mother died. I at the time didn't fully understand the fuss, but now, now I knew what I had missed. The power of my love for my daughter was overwhelming, and as I looked deeply into her eyes reflecting my love for her, I suddenly felt my own loss for the first time. I called my eldest brother as I felt that he may be the only person who might have some understanding of what I was feeling, and from somewhere deep inside, years of loss and grief poured out into the phone. I raged and raged at the injustice, the loss and the sheer tragedy of her death, and for the first time, a level of self-pity entered my soul. How I wished I had a mum in that moment, someone to guide me, to have taught me how to do this, to hold my hand, push back my hair and tell me I was doing great. I was just so angry, and rather than parry each assault, my brother waited patiently until I had exhausted myself, and he said, "Yes, it was a terrible time and a terrible shame, but look at who you are now and what a mother you will be!" I was speechless. In that one statement, I felt completely at peace, and all my self-doubt and insecurities fell away.

Over the coming months and years, she was more than my daughter; she was my inspiration, motivation, and healer. She brought out all the maternal love I had always known I have had, even if I hadn't received any myself. I was always loving, but not like this, as with her, all my many guards came down. I got several things wrong, particularly in the early days, but she was by far the best thing I had ever done to date. I loved every stage of nurturing her through childhood, and now that she is in her early twenties, I can look back and marvel at the miracle of her.

We have an incredible relationship and she has become an amazing young person. We look alike, and yet, also very different. I have fair hair and olive skin; she has dark brown hair and her skin is pure white. She has my mother's Celtic colouring and my grandmother's strength. Her artistic ways are partly from her dad and also from my uncle. She is not at all sporty and finds it hard to even throw a ball, but she is an amazing artist. We have an ease between us and can talk about everything. One of the most impressive things about her is her bravery and commitment to her own truth. The biggest example of this was aged 15 when she told me she was gay.

I was downstairs and received the following:

"Hey mum, just want to let you know that I am not gonna have children because I don't like men. Also, I have been dating my girlfriend now for over 5 ish months Xx"

I really hadn't seen this coming at all but I immediately ran up the stairs to give her the biggest hug and tell her how proud I was. I wanted to know all about her new beau and how she was feeling, but mostly, I just wanted her to experience my love and acceptance. My next thought was to ring her dad. He responded with the very wonderful, "Oh goodie, more women in the house!". I told her this was his reply and she laughed.

Her sexuality is a significant part of who she is, but it's not all of her. She is first and foremost a true artist,and this is who she is, not what she does. I am in awe of her creativity. From the earliest of times, her tiny little fingers were animating some internal impulse to express herself. Whether it be sculpture, watercolour, oil, papier mache, acrylics or whatever comes to hand, she produces the most extraordinary pieces. She has a genuine love of artistic expression and her authenticity and vulnerability are truly awe inspiring. Her passion for art is only rivalled by her love of animals, with cats being her favourite. Her beloved Fidget died recently and it was a huge loss for her. She was just an ordinary black cat rescued from the local centre but she was her world. I would often wander into her room to find Fidget, not just on the bed, but lying across my daughter's chest with the duvet pulled up to her collar.

She is passionate and notably a fierce advocate for the underrepresented and will fire at anyone, including me, should they show any form of bigotry. Calm in a crisis, strong yet nurturing, brave and with true integrity, she's every inch the leader and I'm intrigued as to where this combination of talents will take her.

If pregnancy and birth with my daughter was all

barefoot and bliss, the next pregnancy was all anxiety and discomfort. First off, my battered 33-year-old body was not faring well. I struggled to get up off the floor after my daughter was born due to my back problems which had also affected my pelvis and hips. I was in constant pain, and with a gorgeous (but very demanding) toddler, there was never any time for rest. Then there were the diseases! Whether it was a compromised immune system from general exhaustion or the fact that she brought home more than just arts and crafts from nursery, I caught everything going around; flu, colds, sickness bugs, chest infections, the lot. I was also prone to over-doing things. It wasn't enough to raise a small child, be pregnant with another and run a household, so I signed up for virtually everything and totally over-egged my maternal attentions.

It wasn't just external pressures though; internally things weren't quite right. My midwife, the same one who aided me with my first baby in an elective home delivery, was concerned that my 2nd baby was in a very difficult position to birth. Her advice was to spend as much time as possible on all fours to help turn the baby. My lawn, at the time, was in a terrible state, so I took to spending hours weeding through each section with a small fork-like implement, but to no avail, the baby wouldn't turn. When my due date arrived I was extremely uncomfortable (it was 37 degrees outside), and although I had had day after day of practice contractions, they weren't turning into full-blown labour pains. Practice runs eventually turned into the real thing and by midnight, two weeks after he was scheduled to make an appearance and after 27 hours of very hard labour, my son finally arrived!

He may have been a challenging delivery, but as all mum's know, he was worth all the blood, sweat and tears. My pet name for him when he was a little boy was, "sweetest boy in all the land", which admittedly is a bit of a mouthful. So, over time has been shortened to,"best boy", and has now been abbreviated to "BB", along with his sister who rather unimaginatively of me is BG. Now, I do realise that he is my only boy and she my only girl, and this fact was not lost on him too. He would ask, "How can I be your best boy when you only have one?" This, I had to admit, was a fair point, but I managed to side-step it, given he was only four years old when he first questioned me. I knew I could beat him intellectually at this point! Later, we would get into far deeper discussions, which on occasion, had me whipped. "Who is God's God?" was a good one and led to a lengthy and passionate discussion about evolution. He was about seven for this exchange and over the years we have debated racism, misogyny, communism and most recently, and by far my favourite that he posited, "Is time a real or perceived phenomenon? If it's perceived and time is infinite, then given enough time, surely we can regenerate ourselves as we are just particles at any future or past time with no awareness of time passing". This was a good one and deserved many hours of careful consideration. We can, of course, do small talk, and when we call each other, we go straight into whatever is on our minds without preamble, but our preference is to really get into things, and get into things we do.

As well as having an extraordinary brain, he is blessed with other gifts. First and foremost, he is tall. This was quite the priority for him growing up as he was obsessed with basketball and the wall by the fridge was lacerated by the frequent and desperate growth pen marks. Thankfully, he made it to a very respectable 6ft 2" and basketball continues to be his passion, having played for a national league for most of his teens. He's also a multi-instrumentalist, music producer, film editor and artist, and is currently studying to be an advertising creative at university. I am, of course, very happy that he has so much artistic talent and it remains to be seen what direction he will take, but the thing I most love about him is his character. He has a lovely way about him; always cheerful, eye wateringly funny, naturally chilled and loving. When he puts his long arms around my shoulders, I fall into him and feel so fully connected. He rarely says he loves me, but I don't need words when I can feel and experience it every day in his actions. He puts a lot into this world, and in return, he is much loved by many good people. We have similar tastes in music, film, comedy and tv shows, and if we were superheroes, I would like to think I would be Batman to his Robin, but as I age, perhaps he sees it the other way around!

I will stop there, as I imagine this is coming across a bit much, as all mum's, of course, love their children unconditionally, but not everyone "likes" them too. I really do love and like everything about my children and hope they feel the same in return.

My son may have many natural gifts but life has not always been easy on him. He was born with Iris Coloboma which is a rare congenital defect that mostly affects one eye. However, both of his eyes resemble key holes where the iris has been "interrupted", and therefore not complete. This defect can sometimes be associated with Cat Eye Syndrome, where it goes beyond the more obvious eye presentation and occurs in the heart, kidneys, skeleton, and ears. Over the course of his early years, he was poked and prodded more than most, and although Cat Eye Syndrome was never diagnosed, I believe this affected his confidence in his own health. This is also not helped by his most favourite television show being House MD. Every sprain, pain, sensation or psychological disturbance is analysed to its inevitable conclusion...death! Yep, no matter what it is, it always ends in a self-diagnosed death-sentence of some sort. These prognoses can usually be dismissed with a heavy dose of reassurance from me, but sometimes, words are not enough and a doctor is called, if for nothing else, but to suppress him descending into a nihilistic abyss. I am probably the cause as I am quite the worrier myself and equally infected with the Casandra gene. But, I'd like to think that as I grow older and learn that almost all of the ailments I ever worried about passed without medical intervention, I am beginning to trust that my body is built to last, so long as I don't do anything stupid with it, and I hope that he will come to trust his own too.

I do love being a mum, but as wondrous and intoxicating as motherhood is, it also can come at a heavy price. Women don't generally share how things really are, and certainly in those early interactions with other new mum's, I listened to their tales of how well their cherished child was doing and I felt quite inferior. One memorable issue was my insecurity around vaccinations. My daughter was born in the early 2000's, just as Andrew Wakefield decided to make motherhood even more challenging by asserting that the MMR vaccination had a direct causal link to Autism. I was already struggling with the idea of vaccination long before he put his oar in, so this just lit up my already heightened mental conflict on this issue. Having birthed both my babies at home, with nothing but a postpartum paracetamol, I was committed to the whole breast is best, organic, naturopathic approach to health. So, when at eight weeks it was time to stick a big needle full of goodness knows what into my baby's body, I made it my business to know just about everything there was about immunisation.

Now, ordinarily, this would be considered good parenting. Surely knowing how vaccines work is akin to reading the ingredients of a packet of formula! Well, yes, in one sense, but for me, it was the first foray into the devastating and debilitating phenomena known as thought spiralling. I literally had both sides of the debate raging in my head, morning, noon and night. It consumed all my waking hours and much of my dream state, such that friends were genuinely worried about me as I had become quite the obsessive. With my son's arrival came a new and compounding challenge; he was a hungry baby and wanted almost constant breastfeeding, coupled with a restless toddler, sleep was a distant memory. This went on for months unnoticed as the outside world marvelled at my energy levels. I bought a bicycle made for three, enrolled into daily kids' activities and continued to keep all my social engagements with my new-found mummy friends. On the inside though, things were far from optimal. This only came to light when I finally wrapped my head around vaccination and was visiting the local nurse to begin both children's programmes. Whilst on one of these visits, I turned to the nurse and said, "While I'm here, can you please look at my foot? It's really hurting and I don't have time to re-book to see a doctor?"

I expected the usual, "apply some Savlon and rest a few days", but was greeted with, "You have to go to A&E now!" Thinking she had a touch of the dramatic, I queried this need, but she showed me a red line that was travelling up my calf muscle and said, "This is sepsis and is life threatening. I will call you an ambulance unless you promise me you'll go straight to A&E from here." I agreed to take myself, as I didn't want all the drama, especially with a baby and a toddler in tow.

For some reason though, and this led to further investigation into my state of mind, I went to the walk-in centre and queued alongside everyone else, giving more time for the deadly bacteria to make its way up my body. When I finally told my problem to the nurse, all hell broke loose as several team members rallied to ensure I made it through the day. Massive doses of antibiotics were administered, and once they were satisfied that the red line was receding, I was allowed to go home, but not before the interrogation. "Tell me Julia, what's a typical day for you?",to which I described how I go about my usual mothering duties throughout the day and all through the night. "So when do you sleep?" It was so normalised for me at this point that I didn't feel at all awkward about stating that I just didn't and that this had been since my son's birth, who was now nine months old. In their view, I was clearly in need of help, and over the coming months, I was placed on sleep medication and had close monitoring.

I'm pleased to report that I did eventually get into a sleep routine and that the bacterial infection caused by a tiny piece of glass they found in my heel, cleared up. It was a very close call and I am indebted to the health professionals who took care of me. I recounted this story at the time to a close friend, and she said, "Julia, you MUST take better care of yourself, because if you die, it will be a fucking disaster!" I guess it would have been, but at the time I was so full of preoccupation with my children's health that I had neglected my own, and given how close I was to making them motherless, history could well have repeated itself.

THE ENIGMA PART 2

*B*efore dad finally succumbed to dementia, I made it my business to learn as much about his childhood as I could, in an effort to try and understand him. I knew much of his life within the UK, but through my work in India, I was able to visit his childhood home and school and even meet two of his friends. On one of his lucid days, I told him of my new adventure and he worried that I wouldn't have the constitution for India. But, he needn't have worried because I just loved it, and it was a real joy to share with him all the places and people I had met. His mind eventually shut down forever, two years before his body followed, but before it did, we talked for hours about his birthplace in Colaba, how he loved visiting Bandra, taking strolls along the Apollo Bunder, day trips to Santa Cruz, his school days at Cathedral John Connon, standing awestruck outside but never going in the Taj Mahal Palace Hotel, and on and on the stories went. It was the one thing that was just ours and bonded us like nothing before.

The gap between his mind shutting down whilst his body held on obstinately was very difficult. I couldn't imagine a world without him in it but I also wanted him to die. Through all his hurts, I loved him and couldn't stand watching this once vital, talented, bon viveur, shrivel to a skin-covered skeleton with no functioning consciousness other than a swallowing reflex. I wished him gone so he did not have to live within his useless body and could be free in whatever came next for him. With all that wishing, I was at once shocked and relieved when I finally got the call to say he had passed. My eldest brother was in France at the time and therefore, it fell to me to make all the arrangements. I hurried home, and before I had to deal with all the paperwork, I had the opportunity to sit with him alone. They say you never grow up until you lose both your parents, but as I held his hand, I felt anything but grown-up. I felt like a little lost girl cut adrift from the world; "What am I going to do now dad? I don't know what I'm doing and I need you." I meant every word.

Despite his absence, his presence on the planet kept me grounded, and now he was gone.

He died on June 20th, but his funeral was not until July 15th. With preparations taken care of, there was nothing to do but sit with my grief, which was growing stronger each day; its heavy shroud creeping and crushing with a weight that seemed to drag me deeper into the ground. Grief revealed itself slowly. Distracted by the paramedics who were extremely kind and professional, I focused on paperwork and arrangements as a priority. Having died at home, a coroner had to be called to pronounce him dead. He also needed to be washed and dressed before he could be placed in a black body bag. Once this was done, he was placed on a stretcher and tipped this way and that to navigate through the house and into the private ambulance. All of this, I managed with care, but with a sense of business-like detachment. My sister, on the other hand, was wailing and shrieking and had to be calmed by the paramedics. My middle brother was quite the opposite, in that, he was uncharacteristically quiet which concerned me much more. I made everyone a cup of tea, and once everything was settled, I walked over to my childhood friend's house. I wanted to be with someone who knew me well and would just let me sit. Other friends were in touch that day, and in a perverse parallel with my mum's death, I said nothing as they shared their daily news. When I finally shared the news about my dad's passing, I received the expected, "sorry for your loss" text messages with one or two more expansive replies, but given that he was 90 and had been non-communicative for at least two years, I think his death meant little to most people, as was evident in the reactions of my immediate family and closest friends.

For me, there were some early tears; I met with a close girlfriend and had a good cry, but it was more tension coming out of me than grief, having had to keep myself together for the previous two days. I also had the distraction of a 70th birthday party to attend. It was nice to see everyone but it was hard to get through, so I just smiled and asked them not to talk about my dad. There were work distractions also, so it was some days later that true emotions started to appear.

Anger came first. It began innocently enough; I walked my dog to the local pub and sat in the garden with a drink. The table next to me also had a dog which is always a good conversation opener, so I said hello. The couple chatted happily for a few minutes, and for a moment or so I forgot that I was in the pub alone and that not one of my friends or family were there with me just days after I had lost my very foundations. I had never felt so lonely and rejected, and my ever-present demons started to stir. "I told you; you were kidding yourself, you think all that love you gave out would pay you back? Well, where is everyone now, eh? As I've always told you, you only have yourself to rely upon, and even though you have many people in your life, you are alone in this world"

As this realisation took hold, I had another drink, and then another, and had every intention to go straight back, but en route, I passed another pub. Unlike the previous busy one, this time it was just me. The earlier establishment was quite upmarket and served delicious cocktails but as I sat alone in the relative darkness of a classic boozer, I wanted something cheaper and quicker, so I ordered a shot, then another and another. Maybe it was a mild cry for attention, maybe I thought the barman might ask why a middle-aged woman with a dog was doing mid-afternoon weekday shots, but he just took my order. Several more and I was stumbling home through the woodland. Tears started to appear as the confusing pain of my loss rose within me. My loneliness turned to despair. I went as far as tying up my beloved dog on a busy path so that he might be found before he got too hungry, not sure what I would do or where I would go next. I don't know the exact moment I came to my senses, but it was definitely the thought of my children that shook me. I can't abandon them the way I was abandoned. Shaken, I went back to untie my very baffled but happy dog and went home, hoping that at least if this was a cry for help, my direct family might hear me, and even though subconsciously, I was hoping to be seen. Once home, I made my way to my bedroom avoiding everyone so they would not notice my drunken state. However, my daughter had heard me come upstairs, and finding my locked door, she was crying and begging me to answer. I'd never locked the door before and this was scaring her. I didn't want her to see me in such a state but my need to protect her was stronger than my need to rage into my pillow, so I opened the door. I can only imagine what a sight I was when she saw me, but she just said, "Oh mummy, come here", and as she wrapped her arms around me, my grief poured out in silent shuddering sobs. My daughter, all 16 years of her, knew instinctively that I just needed to be held, and I stayed leant against her for some time until the dark rage started to fade back into the shadows.

The funeral was still some days away, and although my grief was ever-present, I was feeling a lot lighter and turned my attention to honouring my dad. I prepared the most joyous celebration I could, and when everyone was assembled and it was my turn to speak, I delivered flawlessly my tribute to him:

Over the past five years, I had the privilege of spending a great deal of time working in Mumbai - Dad's birthplace and home until his mid-twenties. A vibrant city of colour, light and life. It has intense energy about it, with each day an assault on every sense – a cacophony of car horns, food vendors on every inch of pavement, street markets with their wares strewn across the road, brightly coloured buses and women in the most beautiful saris. A sea of humanity from all social strata, co-existing on the hot dusty streets.

It was a real joy to get to know this wonderful city and to find out more about my dad's life there. I visited his school – Cathedral John Connon, a wonderful colonial building with wooden desks, white uniform and a wonderful central court-yard and is considered the very best school in Mumbai. I went to his childhood home – a modest 4th-floor apartment set in the heart of Colaba near the world-famous Gateway to India. I met his very lovely and very famous childhood friend who became a regular dinner guest of mine and who told me wonderful tales of dad and his other childhood friends.

India shaped my dad in so many ways, his love of animals for example, started there. He told me that he would stop traffic to herd his small flock of ducks from his house to nearby water. Quite a sight I'd imagine, even in the early '30s. Mumbai had and still has many colonial clubs that are very much part of everyday life, and during his late teens and early twenties, this would have been dad's lifestyle with tennis, badminton and cards, all of which became his lifelong passions.

The Hindu faith believes firmly in Karma. Before I went to India, I thought this meant that if you did good deeds, you would move up to a higher level in the next. It does mean this, but it also means that life is outside of your control and that everything is preordained, so just relax and enjoy the day. This is not just a theoretical or spiritual philosophy; it is how life is lived. And this is firmly how dad lived, very much in the moment.

It also shaped how he raised us kids. Dad never drove but would ride his bicycle made for one, with my sister on the handlebars, me on the crossbar and my brother on the back, and my other brother following under his own steam. This is very much the norm in India, albeit on mopeds where a family of five commuting this way is a common sight, not so much in England, but as we know, dad was far from a conformist! He also had very strong views on medicine, which he inherited from his mother; "Beechams powders on the inside and iodine for the out". Given that he took his first antibiotic at 86, I think they may have been onto something, though, I suspect his constitution was another by-product of his Indian past. He also had very strange sayings. Growing up, I thought all kids were called Bevakoof, and it was only later that I realised that this was Hindi for "stupid head". And then, of course, there was his Indian accent, something I had to have pointed out to me as I never noticed it!

Dad was quite a mischief, especially as a boy. My most favourite story was when he was briefly housed in a boarding school. Of course, with such an energetic spirit, he would break out often. On one such breakout, he happened upon a new road being laid with enormous tar barrels placed like sentry guards along the path. I'll let dad take it from here and I'd like you to picture those dazzling blue eyes as he retold his story, "Oh Julia, it was such fun, I went along each one and phut, I knocked them all down. I was very pleased with myself, but when I got back, the headmaster hauled me in front of the whole school and gave me what for on the backside with a cane. Oh, he hit me so hard, but you know what? It was worth it!"

Charming, energetic, convivial, talented, gregarious and irreverent. An irreplaceable one-off that lived life to the full. His legacy is within us four kids, each of us shaped by him in so many ways, as well as his grandchildren who are so far showing great signs of carrying forward his many talents and to whom he was affectionately known as Grandad Chicken. I realise that he was many things to many people over his 90 years, but to me, he was my dad and I am super proud to be his daughter, standing here today, sharing so much of his past. During his declining years, his short-term memory failed him, but he would light up when we spoke of India... something that I got to share with him in the nick of time.

* * *

I would like to say that I worked hard on this speech, that I laboured over every detail and anxiously read and re-read through it ahead of the big day. But the truth is, I wrote it the night before and it flowed out of me whole, as if I had been preparing for it all my life. I knew I wanted to honour his life and share his qualities with the room, but I was also aware that most of them knew him better than that and had sat silently and not so silently through our childhoods, so I didn't want to appear inauthentic. So, my tribute was as much to celebrate his life as to let the room know that yes, he was far from perfect, but perhaps I could try and explain a little of why dad was the way he was. It was also an opportunity for me to let all those people see that I'd turned out okay, but mostly I wanted dad to be proud of me and perhaps even see me the way I wanted him to see me in life - as his advocate, his admirer, his challenger and conscience creator, his judge and his jury who ultimately forgave him. I will never know why he largely abandoned me when I was a child and was ambivalent towards me as an adult, but I do know that I made him proud, and even if he took the credit, I liked it when he boasted about my achievements to others. Now they're both gone and may they rest in peace. One taken tragically, too soon, having never made her mark and the other dying alone, having never remarried. Dad led a full life but he never found love. Yes, there were lovers, but he never found someone to share a life with. I have often wondered how our lives would have been had he been born into a more tolerant time. Perhaps he would have found a man to settle down with, someone to want to make a home with; it would have made all the difference to him and a world of difference to us.

KATHRYN

*T*here are days that change everything. Meeting Kathryn was one such day. I had not been doing well since my dad's funeral. I felt "aggy" like, my clothes didn't fit anymore and my skin was not my own. A dark mood entered my usually sunny disposition and refused to leave, and I was angry at everyone and not sure why. My dad had never been a central relationship even before his dementia robbed him of his mind, so these feelings were confusing. He had not spoken in months, and yet, here I was reeling as if he had died unexpectedly in his prime. This dark brooding went on for weeks and way past the funeral and all its famed powers of closure, so, reluctantly, I sought the help of a counsellor. I say reluctant as I was almost belligerent. It was like someone was making me do it

and I was sulkily agreeing. Even how I chose my counsellor had a certain teenage petulance. Her surname
began with an A, and so, she was top of the list. That
was the extent of my research and I booked my first
session with Donna on an online booking app.

Donna loves to remind me that I entered her beauti-
fully adorned, milky soft-lit office much like a gladiator
entered an arena, in my full business-battle suit, armed
with every avoidance trick in the book and ready to
fight, even though I was going voluntarily to the
contest. She may have been offended by my off handed
ways or perhaps even amused, but she was extremely
patient as I set down my terms of combat. "I will not
talk about my childhood; I've done that to death and
there's nothing anyone can add to this exercise. I will
not engage in anything frivolous or "woo woo". I am
likely to lie to you as I am a total people pleaser. You
will not be able to get anything from me unless I trust
you, which is unlikely, as I will resist being "vulnerable",
and lastly and most noteworthy, I am going to be either
too much or not enough in all aspects of your enquiry,
so, it's probably best we end it here as I don't want to
waste anyone's time". Weeks later, haven broken every
one of the above terms and conditions, I asked her just
how that whole episode was like for her and she just
looked at me directly and said, "When you left, I closed
the door, waited a couple of moments, and out loud

said, "fucking hell, this is gonna be great." And it was great! The next few months we met weekly and got into stuff that I had buried deep. We firstly addressed my marriage. Although a happy one for many years, my husband and I had drifted into that very common territory of "friends". The marriage had just run out of steam and I sat him down and explained that although I will always love him, I wanted a divorce. Donna guided me skilfully over the coming weeks and slowly and carefully, we unravelled 33 years of relationship.

Amongst all of this navigation, we spent quite a lot of time on the subject of my mum. To this day, I struggle to write about her at all. I recently enquired about her medical records as it still troubles me just how she died. I have so many questions and no-one alive to ask, so, I turned to the historical records office to ask for her file. The question itself didn't affect me, what absolutely floored me was the sign off, "I am her daughter". I had never referred to myself in any situation as her daughter and it took my breath away just how powerfully those four words hit me. They replied with what steps I needed to take to get her records, and the list was long and complex which I took as a sign that I shouldn't meddle with whatever was hidden in those documents. My dad recounted many times after my mum's death that a nurse had said she was "black and blue" with bruises and that the autopsy revealed that her organs were unnaturally blackened. This was enough horror for me to deal with, then and now, so I never followed up with the records office. Naturally, we discussed this in one of my weekly sessions along with the ongoing issues with my dad. Somewhere along the line, and I don't say this to be flippant as I literally think my counsellor snuck this in, we talked about sexuality; first, in terms of my dad's and then deftly onto my own. As already covered, women fascinate and alienate me all at once. If I track back, I can give countless examples of emotional paradoxes. From teachers, dinner ladies, early friendships, teenage years, early twenties, and even during my own motherhood, I have been simultaneously drawn to women and wary at the same time. In short, I find them tricky. I had written this off as a lack of mothering and the yearning I had in my body was easily explained as a need for maternal love. This was my stock answer to any question of sexual ambiguity on my part, particularly, given my negative associations with same-gender attraction linked to my dad's hedonistic indulgences. In keeping with my need to be his opposite, I committed to being the most hetero version I could be – husband, kids, mortgage and the lot. My dad had become a powerful kickboard for me to launch into the furthest possible direction. When he died, I had no fight left in me, and it was no coincidence that at this very moment, I was ready to face into what I had always known but had buried so deeply, that only a skilled professional could reveal.

To be exact, my counsellor tricked me. She will maintain that it was an exercise in careful and gentle exploration but I maintain, with heavy sarcasm, that it was a trick! She asked me what I had been watching in the intervening week and I raved about Fleabag. In my head, I am Phoebe Waller Bridge, or better still, that were we to ever meet, she and I would be instant friends. I realise that there are literally millions of women with the same thought as she is truly wonderful. During one of our sessions, having listed all the things I just love about PWB, somewhere out of nowhere I said, "And she has the most beautiful back!" Silence...

"Um, beautiful back?" says my counsellor.

"Yes, don't you think so?" I say, my cheeks burning as if I've just been caught in a lie which I suppose I had.

"Well, it's not a terribly hetero thing to say about another woman," she challengingly said, and I knew I was done for. She proceeded to quiz me on this subject every session. She was mostly subtle, and sometimes not so. She had the bit between her teeth like a puppy with a new toy and no matter how I tried to wrestle the idea from her, she held on tight.

I remember the date. May 25th, 2020. It was just another day in lockdown and of no real significance other than I had my weekly Zoom chat with Donna. Once more, I turned on my laptop, dialled in and got into the usual catch up from the week before. So far, so very standard, and yet today of all days, on the cusp of my 50th year, with no expectation of this momentous moment, she got me to say it. The words did not come easily. I started with a percentage split. Afterall, I had been with a man for so many years and enjoyed a full marriage with all its intimacies, so surely, this allows me some sort of ambiguity. I've also had my fair share of celebrity crushes with James McAvoy and Ralph Fiennes particularly high on the list. Okay, yes, in every screen kiss, I watched the woman's lips; yes, I had many girl crushes growing up; yes, I watched Orange is the New Black mostly so I could watch Piper and Alex make out and yes, PWB really does have an amazing back, but so what!? I hung onto at least a 70/30 split for much of the session, but in the end, like a beleaguered MMA fighter, I tapped out. "Ok, ok, I'm Gay! Are you happy now?" She was ecstatic and I was exhausted. In that moment, years and years of self-denial, avoidance and downright self-subjugation came to an end. The genie was firmly out of the bottle and my counsellor had thrown away the cork.

Her first bit of advice was that I tell people closest to me. I started with my two best girlfriends. Yvon is my soul sister. We look like sisters and act like them too. There's nothing I can't say to Yvon or thought I couldn't until I had to discuss my newfound sexual identity. Having clumsily delivered the message, her first question was a playful "ooh, did you ever fancy me?" She was momentarily crestfallen, given that she was only asking out of ego, so when I said, "of course not, you are my sis, so stop being weird", I imagine she was rather put out. But in truth, even though she is an attractive woman, I never did because it really doesn't work like that, in the same way that not every man in my life should wonder about my attraction to him prior to my revelation. Over the coming days, I tested the water with several nearest and dearest, but the big conversations were still ahead of me. First up, was Kate. Our friendship has endured through so much of life's joys and trials. We are very close and yet in all these years, I have never shared any thoughts on this subject, so, when I sat her down in front of me with a sincerity that she's not witnessed before, and said, "I have something to tell you", she cried, "oh my God, you're not ill are you?" Having reassured her that I was perfectly fine, and then delivering the news, she responded in typical Kate style. Before the sentence had barely left my mouth, she was into action mode; "well, you're gonna have to figure out how the gay scene works. Hmmm, who do I know that's gay? Oh, I know…. you must meet Kathryn. She's lovely and will help for sure", and with that, she'd texted her to ask if she'd talk to me.

I was a little nervous in the build up to talking with Kathryn but I needn't have been. We talked over the phone for almost an hour and she was so reassuring. Now in her early forties, she'd come out at the age of 23 when she'd met her current wife. She explained that they were probably not going to be the best guides as they live a quiet married life and were not part of any "scene" as such, but if I would like to meet up and talk through anything, they would be happy to have me over. It was mid June and the sun was shining, so, we agreed to have drinks in their garden in a few days' time.

I arrived at their address with a bottle of fizz in my hand which was left over from my 50th birthday festivities. It seemed fitting to share a bottle with my newfound friends and celebrate my first tentative steps into this brave new world. With a little trepidation, I rang the bell and waited, but there was nothing. Oh no! Perhaps I've got the wrong address, or worse still, Kathryn had ghosted me and was only talking to me on the phone to appease Kate. My mind was racing but I pushed the bell once more in the hope that my paranoia would be just that. Still nothing. I was just about to turn away when I heard, "hello lovely! Oh sorry, have you been standing there long?" Out from the side of the house Kathryn leant from the gable of the side door. I'm not exactly sure what I was expecting but I can say with certainty that I wasn't expecting the person in front of me. Tall, blonde and with a beautiful smile, she was stunning, and she welcomed me into her garden and apologised profusely for keeping me waiting.

I was introduced to her wife whom I recognised at once as we'd gone through the same schools, although, I think she was a year or two ahead of me. We talked amiably for several hours and it was so good to share my history with them both. Her wife had a very different experience, in that, she'd always been "out", but Kathryn and I shared the same slow burning realisation, having once dated men. So, we understood the confusion that this brings, both within oneself and also with those who have grown to associate you with male relationships. Through the whole conversation, I just felt completely at peace, like I'd more than come out, I'd come home.

Over the coming weeks, Kathryn and I would meet up and walk our dogs together. She had a gorgeous "little fluffer" which was a mix of Bichon and Poodle. I had the less designer Beagle varieties, one of which I'd had since a pup and was now almost 16 and another that I'd rescued just a short while before and was still getting to know. At first, our conversations centred around her coming out; what I could learn from her experience, particularly with telling friends and family, and what I could expect in terms of dynamics between same-sex relationships. She shared her admittedly narrow understanding of online dating as well as a limited idea of what bars I might find helpful. Mostly, though, we talked about her family, and in particular, her mum's recent Leukaemia diagnosis. She was naturally very worried and much of our walks and talks centred around her hopes and fears. Slowly, though, she started to share some of the cracks in her marriage. She was extremely respectful and took great care not to say anything too critical but as weeks passed, it was becoming clear to me that things were not right. Some of the things she shared were very alarming; even more shocking was what I would witness directly.

On another balmy evening, this time sitting on an outside table at a local pub chatting amiably, her wife suddenly produced a set of property details and tried to pitch to us all about its various merits. Kathryn quietly argued that this was not at all what she wanted and gave numerous reasonable opinions as to why. I assumed this was all a work in progress and here were two people discussing possibilities, but then, her wife announces that she had made an offer and it had been accepted. I'm not sure who was more stunned, me, or the other parties at the table but curiously, Kathryn didn't protest; she just sat quietly as the topic moved on.

It was at this moment that I knew I couldn't be friends with them both. Everyone I had met until that moment had always talked about them as a double act. Kathryn had one friend of her own but mostly, their friends regarded them as a package deal. I called Kathryn the next morning to say that I was looking forward to seeing her when I got back from my holiday but maybe just for occasional dog walks as I found last night's conversation a little difficult. She said that she'd noticed that I wasn't my usual chatty self. I shared a little of what I thought about the house buying but not too much, as it was not my place. I wished her well and left it at that.

I settled into my holiday with the kids, and although I was distracted by daily comings and goings, Kathryn was often on my mind. I wondered how she was, whether the house had gone through, whether she was out walking alone now with her dog as her wife was never keen to join her. I was out with my own dogs when I received a text from her wife, asking me to keep away, no more dog walks, no more anything and not to make contact with Kathryn. My first instinct was to text back saying that I was free to contact whomever I choose, as is Kathryn, but I calmed down and called Kate who was there the last time we all met, and I wondered if we'd upset her by challenging the house purchase plan. Kate was very clear, "it's not going to be about the house, it's going to be about you", but I disagreed. I was sure that it was going to be about the house and texted her wife apologising if I had over-stepped in any way. She confirmed Kate's suspicions and blasted back that her marriage is now over and it was all my fault. I knew Kathryn liked me and I was certainly becoming very protective of her, so maybe she was right; at the very least, something must have been said, otherwise why the angry text?

Reluctantly, I did as I was told and made no contact with Kathryn. I surmised that whatever was happening, it was best if I kept my distance. Three days passed and then I received a text from Kathryn. She apologised for her wife's texts and explained that things had not been good for a while and that I had inadvertently walked into a marriage in crisis. I said that I was sorry to hear this and asked her if she was okay and if she needed me to do anything. She reassured me that she was fine and that they just needed time to work things out, and that she would get back in touch with me when I got back in a week or two.

On my return, we agreed to meet up for another dog walk.

Kathryn kept it light at first, not wanting to get into anything and I respectfully didn't pry. As we passed close to the café in the centre of the walk, she brought up the house purchase. Her wife was still pressing ahead and she wanted my opinion. I was quiet for a moment or two then shared that I couldn't advise anymore as I was compromised. She pushed me on this point and I said, "I couldn't be impartial as I, I, well I, I am starting to have feelings for you". I'm usually articulate, but these words fell out of my mouth as if I had dropped a tray full of beer glasses and was hopelessly flailing around trying to catch them. Up until this moment, I had no idea what had really gone on, I had no idea if Kathryn "like-liked" me, and I had been practising vulnerability with Donna, but I was really out there with this one. I could barely look at her and held my breath in case I had blown it, but at that moment, she lightly touched my shoulder, turned me toward her and said, "I think about you all the time".

Now, in the film of our love story, I want Cate Blanchett playing Kathryn and Kate Winslet playing me. Cate would deliver this line with such intense sensuality, much like Kathryn did, and Kate would sweep her into her arms and land the perfect screen kiss, along with some killer line to rival anything the film Jerry Maguire could muster. In real life, what actually happened was me play-thumping her on her shoulder, like a schoolboy being asked out on a first date, followed by a goofy, "really! Me!?" We walked side by side for some time, both stunned by what had just passed between us. It was sometime later, walking side by side, that I felt it again – a magnetic tractor beam drawing our hands closer together as we ambled along a woodland track. I turned at one point and asked her if she was okay, as her face was flushed and she looked a little unwell. We continued a short way ahead and she asked if I was okay, and from somewhere quite unfamiliar, I said, "I'm okay, but I'd really like to hold your hand", to which she turned to me once more, placed her hand on the small of my back, pulled me in close and kissed me. And what a kiss it was! It was as if the Gods had all aligned and sent a lightning bolt through my head. It was as if, everyone who had ever loved me was now looking down on this woodland scene and were cheering. It was as if every earthly thing had collided then reversed to force time to stop, just for a moment, so I could take it all in. Once again, in the movie, Kate Winslet would say something sensual and powerful. I, on the other hand, having steadied myself against a tree, looked up shyly and said, "can we do that again?", and we did.

What followed deserves its own 3-part Netflix series. First there was the split. Her ex-wife would not accept that the marriage was over and started her campaign, firstly, with love bombing, and when that didn't work, then came the threats and intimidation, soon followed by hacking into Kathryn's phone and reading all her messages from me and then loading them into her written and verbal assaults. Not satisfied with her private attacks, she then took to social media. I have never been trolled before. In fact, I've hardly experienced a bad word said to me in any medium, barring a few disgruntled ex-employees, grumbling about their untimely exit. That said, I was surprisingly calm as I saw my face splashed all over Kathryn's social media accounts, denouncing me as a wife stealer. I think her now ex had hoped to shame me, or perhaps, "out" me, but achieved neither. I had already come out to my nearest and dearest, including my ex-husband and my kids, so this held no power over me. And I most certainly didn't feel shame. I wished she and Kathryn could have sorted things out months ago when I received the first round of texts but I didn't feel any direct accountability for the dissolution of their marriage, which had started years before. I feel for her ex though. Kathryn really is irreplaceable and I hope she can find love again to help her heal. I feel for Kathryn too as she is a good person. She tried to end her marriage with grace well before THE KISS! But, it takes two to tango as the saying goes, and her ex would not allow her to leave as she would have liked.

The second episode would centre on the tentative steps that Kathryn and I took to form our new relationship. She really is a remarkable woman; that exquisite mix of outer beauty and inner strength that I never knew I needed, until she pulled me into her and has held me safe ever since. More than this, I now know what true partnership means. It's having someone in your life that's truly yours. She is my constant companion; my cheerleader, sofa-sharer, bed-warmer, pain-taker, home-maker and joy-creator. She makes me feel home wherever we are and I sleep soundly next to her, knowing that I don't have to take on life alone and that whatever happens, we will sort things out together. She is my person and I can't imagine life without her.

In the TV adaptation, viewers would watch enrapt, as Cate Blanchett and Kate Winslet assembled furniture in Cate's new pad. They would watch tearfully as they celebrated their first Christmas together with friends and family. They would laugh joyously as they saw all their tender and funny little ways and would cheer as they slowly forged two lives into one. In real life, the ex would continue to wriggle and writhe, but as the months moved on, she would fade into the background, with us both wishing her well and hoping too, that she might find love again and leave us alone from here.

And so, to the final episode.

Well, it has yet to be written. My hope is that it is filled with a love story of two women who lived almost parallel lives just 2 miles apart; content, but not fulfilled, and who now spend each day growing deeper and deeper in love. I hope Kate Winslet can pull out an Oscar performance and emote a lifetime of yearning, finally broken by her meeting the love of her life and falling into the arms of Cate Blanchett who needs to bring her career best to live up to Kathryn. The closing montage will be a pin board of parties, travels, dog walks and our shared lives full of love and laughter until we are old and grey. I promised my son I would live until 103. Kathryn is a little younger, so I'm afraid she'll have to die at just 96 as we've agreed to go together. We are, of course, just playing, but in principle, she's fine with this idea so long as I go first. I'm totally fine with that too. In fact, we have rehearsed our death scene on many an occasion. It's a little macabre to do this but somehow it makes the inevitable feel less scary. With great love, there is always heartbreak, so, given that one of us will find ourselves alone, it is somehow comforting to fool around with the idea.

The following script is my best attempt to re-enact one of our impromptu skits around this subject. It is fairly accurate, particularly in that I tend to talk a lot and Kathryn is very patient. It is, of course, heavily laced with sarcasm, and as you can see from the following script, her patience is tested right to the very end…

* * *

Me/Kate W: I've always loved you. You are my everything. I know we met late in life but I wouldn't change a thing, and I feel so blessed that we've had the second half to live life authentically. I never could have imagined just how powerful it was to live wholeheartedly the way we have, and I'm so very thankful.

Kathryn/Cate B: Yes baby, I know. I love you too, now go into the light. Come on, it's time.

Me/Kate W: But I'm not ready to go yet. I have so much more I want to say. You are such a beautiful soul. So kind, generous, patient and true. All this mixed with a wicked sense of fun and mischief and coupled with your inner and outer beauty. I really can't believe my good fortune.

Kathryn/Cate B: Aw thank you, as I said, I love you too. (to the children who are gathered at my bedside) Now mummy is fading darlings, it's time to say goodbye.

. . .

Me/Kate W: (closes her eyes and breathes slow shallow breaths, but then....) No baby, you don't understand, (all three assembled roll their eyes) I love you! With all my heart. I always said I would either be too much or not enough, but with you, I was just right. It was just right. You made me full to the brim, and all that I am, I credit to you. Everything I have achieved, I credit to you. You are my soulmate and I want you to know that.

Kathryn/Cate B: I know baby, you've said as much many times over the past 53 years. Now come on, Waitrose closes soon.

Me/Kate W: Ok, here I go. I'm going....to.....the.... light....................(her breath slows to almost nothing, there is an expectation in the room, everyone holds hands and waits for the final passing, and yet, with one last gasp and with all her strength, she rises from the bed like a zombie, propelled forward from the hips) one last thing.....I used to be a CEO you know!

Kathryn/Cate B: (exasperated but tender) Yes baby, you were. Now off you pop. I'll be right behind you...

ACKNOWLEDGMENTS

I am eternally grateful to the friends, family and colleagues that gave such valuable feedback, particularly with the early drafts. Special thanks to Dilys Denney, Kate Gulliver, Donna Arnold, Ann Phillips, Adam Quig, Vips Larsen, Michelle Sharp, Ksenia Kokareva, Darryl Duthie, Joanna Brown, Kathy Ren, Yvon Payne and Fran Gill. I would like to thank the team at Odd Marble ApS that brought the book to life, especially, Rikke Hundal for leading the whole enterprise and ensuring the very best outcome, and Sharon Vanessa for her expert editing skills. Lastly, I would like to thank Kathryn for her constant and thoughtful insights throughout the creation of "Dogbone" and for loving the "little ragamuffin" within it.

ABOUT THE AUTHOR

Julia lives in Surrey with her two children, her partner Kathryn and her Beagle, Brodie. Over the years, she has both built and led numerous businesses, has been an artist and nurtured other artists in the competitive world of the music industry. She has also had the privilege of living and working in the US and India. Given she started her career at a local leisure centre; a job she took in order to use its laundry facilities to wash her own clothes, her origin story is something of an enigma.

E-mail: houseondogbonestreet@gmail.com

facebook.com/thehouseondogbonestreet
instagram.com/thehouseondogbonestreet

Printed in Great Britain
by Amazon

27419020R00118